DECORATING YOUR GARDEN

DECORATING YOUR GARDEN

A Bouquet of Beautiful & Useful
Craft Projects to Make & Enjoy

BY MICKEY BASKETT

Sterling Publishing Co., Inc.
New York

Prolific Impressions Production Staff:

Editor: Mickey Baskett
Photography: Jeff Herr, Jerry Mucklow, Miche Baskett
Copy: Miche Baskett
Graphics: Dianne Miller, Michael Moore
Styling: Susan Mickey, Laney McClure
Proofing: Jim Baskett

Library of Congress Cataloging-in-Publication Data
Baskett, Mickey.
    Decorating your garden / Mickey Baskett.
        p.   cm.
    Includes index.
    ISBN 0-8069-9443-6
    1. Handicraft. 2. Garden ornaments and furniture. I. Title.
  TT157.B35 1998
  745.5--dc21   97-43001
                                 CIP

10 9 8 7 6 5 4 3 2

First paperback edition published in 1999 by
Sterling Publishing Company, Inc.
387 Park Avenue South, New York, N.Y. 10016
© 1998 by Prolific Impressions, Inc.
Distributed in Canada by Sterling Publishing
% Canadian Manda Group, One Atlantic Avenue, Suite 105
Toronto, Ontario, Canada M6K 3E7
Distributed in Great Britain and Europe by Cassell PLC
Wellington House, 125 Strand, London WC2R 0BB, England
Distributed in Australia by Capricorn Link (Australia) Pty Ltd.
P.O. Box 6651, Baulkham Hills, Business Centre, NSW 2153, Australia

Printed in China
All rights reserved

Sterling ISBN 0-8069-9443-6 Trade
         0-8069-9470-3 Paper

CONTENTS

6

INTRODUCTION

8

PLACING YOUR GARDEN ART

16

MOSAICS FOR THE GARDEN

30

OUTDOOR PAINTED ART

70

GARDEN SIGNS

80

DOOR MATS

86

BIRDIE BED & BREAKFAST

104

FLOWERPOTS WITH FLOURISH

110

WHIRLIGIGS & WHIMSY

120

ANTIQUES IN THE GARDEN

126

INDEX

INTRODUCTION

Your garden is a place where you can indulge in the calm, quiet beauty of the outdoors. It is also an extension of your home, that can be enhanced with a touch of creative decoration. This book provides ideas and techniques for a variety of art projects to make for your garden. It also will show you how to arrange and display your garden art. With the easy step-by-step instructions included here you can make over thirty projects and also learn a lot of fun techniques for creating outdoor furniture, fence, sign, and patio painting, flower pot decorations, birdhouse making, and mosaic making which you can use to design even more of your own garden art.

This book features the best in contemporary garden art. Eight different designers have contributed their talents to give you a variety of beautiful, fun-to-make projects for your garden. Make the outside of your home as lovely and personalized as the inside, and enjoy the process!

CHAPTER 1

PLACING YOUR GARDEN ART

With careful placement of your decorations and art, you can create a beautiful outdoor garden gallery.

Bren Kyle made the most of her shady back yard by converting a rarely-used swimming pool into a beautiful garden pond. A canopy of tree-tops creates a ceiling overhead. The canopy helps to make the garden feel like an outdoor living area, another room of the home. With the pond as the centerpiece, Bren has turned her garden into a gallery for outdoor art. As visitors walk around the pond, a path leads them from one point of interest to another and each new focal point combines the beauty of garden flowers and greenery with the creative touch of Bren's decorations.

Throughout the garden, many of the birdhouses Bren creates for resale are featured. Their rustic charm and touches of whimsey make them a focal point to any setting.

Finished birdhouses in this chapter were created by Bren Kyle, Decatur, Georgia.

Garden Created by Bren Kyle

CREATING VIGNETTES

Without walls, corners, hallways, or windows to guide you, knowing where to place your garden art can be difficult. Randomly scattering it throughout the garden can clutter the garden, detract from the beauty of the flowers, and overwhelm your eyes as you try to look at everything. Try creating small areas of interest, or vignettes, throughout the garden.

Bren often uses furniture as a way of displaying her garden art. The photo on this page shows how she has placed a bench along the path. Using the bench, not as a seat, but rather as a focal point and display for her art, she now has a small area of interest.

Continuing along the path, you can see in the photo on the opposite page how Bren has placed her art in a cluster together against a fence. This is another vignette, with the fence as the backdrop and the birdhouses as the focal point. Again she has used furniture to display the decorations. The large wreath (about four feet diameter) serves as a frame for her hand-made birdhouses.

USING FENCES FOR HANGING YOUR ART

A fence around your garden provides the perfect space for hanging decorations. You can hang hand-made projects, planters, or antique signs.

The photo on the opposite page shows how Bren has created another vignette using a fence to enclose the area of interest. A small pond placed along the fence is highlighted by the decorations hanging along the fence. A window-shaped mirror with a planter makes a wonderful addition to a fence.

HANGING YOUR ART ON TREES

Using trees to display your garden art is a nice way to integrate the natural living creatures of your garden with your handmade items. You can place your decorative pieces at all different levels, encouraging visitors to pull their eyes up away from the ground and notice the beauty of the taller garden dwellers.

When hanging art on a tree, use a long screw instead of a nail. As the tree grows, you can back out the screw and continue using it. A nail will be swallowed by the bark of a growing tree.

VIEWS OF THE GARDEN

Your garden is much more than your backyard. It is an outdoor living space and an extension of your home. When thinking of your garden as an extension of your home, you begin to realize how it can enhance your inside living areas. A well-placed garden or a few well-placed windows give you a view of your garden from the inside which can significantly brighten up the interior of your home.

Bren's garden creates a wonderful, peaceful mood for the patio on the back of her house. The patio is the perfect entry way to the garden, a bridge between outdoor and indoor. It also provides another wonderful opportunity for displaying garden art.

This photo shows a view from Bren's living room, looking out towards the garden. Her garden can be enjoyed even from the inside because of the large windows.

CHAPTER 2

MOSAICS FOR THE GARDEN

Mosaics are bright, lively, and a lovely addition to your outside areas. Also, they are sturdy enough to withstand a lot of use and weather wear. Although they look detailed and complex, mosaics are not very difficult to make. You will love the fun you can have working with the bright colors and simple shapes. The techniques for making mosaics require very few materials and can be done within a few hours (not including drying time). You could apply the techniques you learn here and create a multitude of garden accessories.

This chapter teaches you general skills for making mosaics and then tells you everything you need to know to make several garden decorations and accessories, including stepping stones and a table. You will learn how to create the tile pieces and then place them onto the project surface.

The most important ingredient for making mosaics is the mosaic tiles and pieces, which are readily available. Small tiles in a variety of sizes are available and ready to use. Also, you can collect old china plates, pottery, glass, and tiles from flea markets and then break them into pieces yourself. After you have collected your mosaic pieces, lay them out into a design of your choice. The design can be your own or one that you find in this book or a variety of other sources. When you have decided on a design, you then glue your mosaic pieces onto the project surface, which can be almost anything that you dream up: wood furniture, a bird-bath, plaques & signs, terra cotta pots, etc. . . By filling in the spaces between the mosaic pieces with sand-free grout, you've completed your mosaic!

Mosaic Stepping Stones:
See page 24 for instructions.

MATERIALS FOR CREATING MOSAICS

For creating mosaics, you will need the following materials (pictured starting top left and moving clockwise):

Premixed tile grout (sand-free) for filling the space between mosaic pieces

Glass nippers for cutting china and pottery to make mosaic pieces

Broken china to use as mosaic pieces

A variety of ceramic tiles to use as mosaic tile pieces

Rubber spatula for applying grout between the mosaic pieces

All-purpose white glue for attaching mosaic pieces and tiles to project surface

PROJECT SURFACES

You can create mosaics using almost any surface as a base for your project. Mosaics look wonderful added to **concrete pieces** such as stepping stones, bird-baths, or furniture; **wood pieces** such as plaques and signs; **terra cotta pots**; or **metal pieces** such as a mailbox. Find old pieces of furniture to decorate and rejuvinate with your mosaic art or purchase project pieces from home stores, craft stores, and even flea markets.

MOSAIC PIECES

To make mosaics, you will need **broken pieces of glass, china, pottery, or tiles**. You can purchase old china plates, pottery, glass, and tiles at flea markets and then break them into pieces. Finding brightly colored plates or plates with designs can greatly enhance your mosaic designs.

You can also purchase **ceramic tiles** in different shapes, sizes, and colors at home supply stores and some craft stores. These combine nicely with pottery and china and can help give structure to your design.

TOOLS

You will need **newspaper or a paper bag and a rubber mallet, hammer, and safety glasses** for breaking ceramic, china, glass, and pottery pieces. After you break the pieces with the mallet, you can use **glass nippers** to cut the pieces smaller and into a variety of shapes.

A **rubber spatula or a nylon trowel** is needed for spreading grout onto surface.

To plan your mosaic design, you will need **paper, a pencil, and scissors.** If you choose to use a pattern, you may also need **graphite transfer paper.**

GLUE

To assemble your mosaic, you need all-purpose white glue to attach the mosaic pieces to the project surface.

GROUT

After all the pieces are glued into place, you will fill in the spaces between the pieces with sand-free tile grout. You can use a premixed sand-free grout or a dry sand-free grout. To use the dry grout, mix it with water until it is an icing consistency.

FINISH

After the grout has dried, you can seal your project for outdoor use. Use either a spray or brush-on sealer that is made for outdoor use and apply at least two coats.

HOW TO CREATE MOSAICS

1

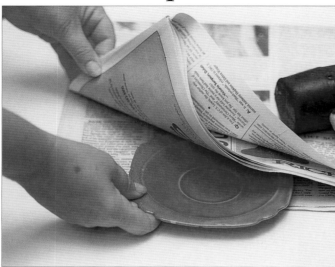

2

Prepare surface (for wood projects only):

Wood projects require some preparation. However, most other surfaces do not and you may begin creating your mosaic as the first step.

1. If creating a mosaic on a wood surface, you will need to first sand the wood and wipe away the dust.
2. Coat the wood with primer using a sponge brush.
3. You may wish to paint the edges of the project surface at this time. Apply two coats and allow to dry thoroughly.

Plan design:

4. Trace the project surface onto a piece of paper and cut out the tracing to make a template.
5. If you would like to create a design with the mosaic pieces, you can sketch a design onto your template. If you are using a pattern, transfer the pattern onto your template with graphite transfer paper. You may also choose to lay the mosaic pieces out in a random design. Therefore, not needing to sketch the design.

3

4

NOTE: Sketching your own design can be fun, but it can also be just as enjoyable to find designs to use as patterns. Sources for designs include stencils, graphic arts books, clip art books, or anywhere you might find a simple design.

Prepare the mosaic pieces:

6. To break old china or pottery into pieces, first place plates or pottery, one at a time, between several layers of newspaper or in a paper bag. See photo #1. Wear safety glasses.
7. Use a rubber mallet to break plates or pottery into pieces. See photo #2.

8. Break smaller pieces off china and pottery with glass nippers. Also use glass nippers to create straight edges on pieces or to shape pieces so that they will fit into your pre-planned design. See photo #3.

Assemble the mosaic:

9. Lay mosaic pieces out onto your paper template, forming your design and planning the position of each mosaic piece.

5

6

10. Use all-purpose white glue or mastic to attach mosaic pieces, half marbles, or ceramic tiles to project surface as they are laid out on the paper template. Work in small sections at a time. See photo #4.
11. Allow all glue to dry.
12. If using dry grout, prepare it by mixing it with water to an icing consistency. You may also purchase it premixed.
13. Spread premixed tile grout over the project surface using a rubber spatula. Make sure to push the grout into the spaces between tiles. See photo #5.
14. Allow to dry for 10 - 15 minutes.

15. While grout is still wet, use a damp sponge or rag to wipe grout off tops of mosaic pieces. Rinse sponge in a bowl of water frequently. See photo #6.
16. Allow grout to dry another 10 minutes. You should see a white haze over the mosaic pieces. Wipe this away with a damp rag or towel. Allow grout to dry 4 - 6 hours.

Finish:
17. Use spray or brush-on outdoor sealer to seal your project. Follow manufacturer directions for sealer application. ✣

Tabletop Elegance

Created By Connie Sheerin

Display this table anywhere in your garden for a touch of elegance in the outdoors. Imagine serving an icy pitcher of lemonade in the middle of summer to your garden guests. They would not be able to place their glasses down on this beautiful work of art without noticing your attention to detail in your garden. Functional and delightful!

Supplies Needed

Project surface:

Round wooden table top, 19" diameter x 3/4" thick
Table legs or stand of your choice

For preparing wood:

Sandpaper
Wood primer
Sponge brush

For preparing design:

Paper & pencil
Scissors

For preparing mosaic pieces:

200 square mini ceramic tiles, 1/2": black, ochre, gray, beige
4 - 5 dozen square glass tiles, 1": teal, white, tan with metallic
16 half marbles: turquoise and amber
Stained glass pieces: beige, tan, amber, teal, turquoise, blush, spruce, peach, and yellow ochre
Glass nippers
Safety glasses

For assembling & finishing:

Lazy Susan (optional)
All-purpose white glue
Sand-free tile grout
Sponge
Bowl
Outdoor sealer

Here's How

Prepare wood:

1. Lightly sand all wood. Wipe away dust.
2. Coat wood with primer using a sponge brush.

Plan design:

3. Make a paper template of table top as explained in general instructions.
4. Sketch a design in the middle of the table top as shown in picture. This design was traced from a stencil pattern.

Prepare mosaic pieces:

5. While wearing safety glasses, break stained glass into pieces as explained in general instructions.
6. Use glass nippers to cut stained glass into small pieces and a variety of shapes. Also cut pieces to fit the design on the template.

Plan the mosaic pattern:

7. Use the paper template to plan mosaic, working around the design in the center. First, spread out paper template.
8. Place stained glass pieces on template to create center design.
9. Place 1" glass tiles around outer edge of template, inserting a half marble between every three tiles. Alternate colors as shown in photo.
10. Place mini tiles around template at the next row inward, alternating colors as shown in photo.
11. Fill the remaining area of the template between the center design and the outside rows of tiles with pieces of stained glass. Space the shapes and colors evenly throughout the template.

Assemble & finish:

12. *Optional:* Place table top on Lazy Susan to make working on the surface easier. You will not need to move around the table.
13. Glue mini tiles around outside rim of table top. Place them about 1/4" away from each other and alternate colors as shown in photo.
14. Glue remaining tiles and glass pieces on table top as they are laid out on the paper template. Work in small sections at a time. Allow all glue to dry.
15. Prepare grout and apply to table top edge and surface according to general instructions. Allow to dry and wipe away following general instructions.
16. Use a small dry stencil brush to add copper paint to mosaic pieces in center design.
17. Seal entire table top according to manufacturer's directions on sealer, making sure to brush or spray sealer over all mosaic pieces and grout. Allow to dry.
18. Attach legs to table top.

STEPPING INTO COLOR

Created By Kathi Malarchuk

These mosaic stepping stones are a wonderful way to add color to the green areas of your garden. Concrete stepping stones of many shapes and sizes can be purchased at garden shops or hardware and home stores. They are then easily enhanced with either a mosaic of a planned design such as the floral stone shown or a random pattern.

SUPPLIES NEEDED

Project surface:
Concrete stepping stones, 12" x 12" (available at garden shops or hardware and home stores)

For planning design:
Paper & pencil
Scissors

For preparing mosaic pieces:
Old ceramic plates, 2 - 3 per stepping stone: blue, yellow, pink, green, and gray used here (available at flea markets)
Mallet or hammer
Newspaper or paper bag
Glass nippers
Safety glasses

For assembling & finishing:
Premixed gray tile mastic for exterior use, 1 pint
White sand-free tile grout, 1 pint when mixed
Grout sealer
Trowel
Rubber spatula
Sponge or rags
Blank paper, 12" x 12"

HERE'S HOW

Plan design and prepare pieces:
1. Draw a template of the stepping stones as explained in general instructions.
2. You may create a random design or plan a flower design as pictured.
3. Insert plates, one at a time, into newspaper or paper bag. Wear safety glasses and use mallet to break plates into small pieces.
4. Lay mosaic pieces onto paper template to plan your design.

Assemble mosaic:
5. Apply mastic to top of stepping stones with a trowel following mastic manufacturer's instructions. Insert mosaic pieces into mastic following design on template. Allow to dry for 24 hours.
6. If using dry grout, prepare it by mixing it with water to an icing consistency. You may purchase it premixed.
7. Spread premixed tile grout over mosaic using a rubber spatula. Allow to dry and wipe away grout following general instructions.

Finish:
8. Apply grout sealer to stones according to manufacturer's instructions. Allow to dry for 48 hours before use. 🐝

HOW'S THE WEATHER?

Created By Connie Sheerin

This Barometer was created using a random pattern for mosaic piece placement. However, some of the tiles used are hand-made as a way of personalizing the design. These hand-made tiles are optional. Just as they could be left off of this project, they could be added as a fun new element to your other mosaic projects. To learn how to make your own tiles, see specific instructions for making tiles.

SUPPLIES NEEDED

Project surface:
Wooden plaque with cut-out for barometer, 10" x 6-1/2"
Barometer, 3"

For preparing wood:
Sandpaper
Wood primer
Acrylic craft paint: metallic antique gold
Sponge brush
Flat brush

For making mosaic pieces from clay, optional:
Polymer clay: black
Rolling pin
Rubber stamps of words or patterns of your choice
Gold bronzing powder
Craft knife
Cardboard
Brush-on high-gloss finish

For preparing mosaic pieces:
Mini ceramic tiles: black
12 -14 square glass tiles, 1": teal with metallic
2 old china plates with patterns
Rubber mallet
Newspaper or paper bags
Glass nippers
Safety glasses

For assembling & finishing:
All-purpose white glue
Sand-free tile grout
Rubber spatula
Bowl
Sponge
Paper & pencil
Scissors
Small brush
Brush-on sealer

HERE'S HOW

Prepare wood:
1. Lightly sand wood plaque. Wipe away dust.
2. Coat plaque with primer using a sponge brush. Allow to dry.
3. Paint border around plaque with two coats of gold paint, allowing to dry between coats.

Prepare mosaic pieces:
4. Place china plates, one at a time, between layers of newspaper or in a paper bag and break with a mallet. Wear safety glasses.
5. Use glass nippers to cut plate pieces smaller (about 1/2 inch - 1 inch pieces) in a variety of shapes.
6. Use glass nippers to cut tiles into assorted shapes.
7. Make your own tiles if desired.

Plan mosaic design:
8. Trace plaque onto paper and cut out tracing to use as a template.
9. Place tiles and mosaic pieces on template, planning the design.

Assemble & finish:
10. Glue barometer into plaque.
11. Glue tiles and mosaic pieces onto plaque as they are laid out on template. Allow glue to dry.
12. Prepare grout and apply to surface according to general instructions. Allow to dry and wipe off as explained in general instructions.
13. Retouch gold paint on plaque if necessary.
14. Use a small brush to apply sealer to project, avoiding barometer and clay tiles. Apply two coats. ✀

MAKE YOUR OWN CLAY TILES

With these Supplies:

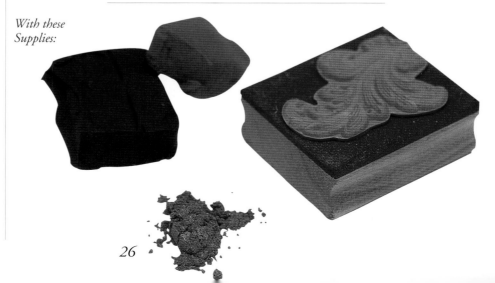

HOW TO MAKE YOUR OWN CLAY TILES

Supplies

You can easily make your own tiles to personalize your mosaics. To do so you will need cardboard, a craft knife, a rolling pin, an oven, high-gloss finish, and the following pictured items (starting top left, moving clockwise):

Polymer clay (comes in an array of colors and bakes quickly in your own oven)

Rubber stamps for creating designs on the tiles

Gold bronzing powder for rubbing on the tiles to make the stamped designs show more brilliantly

Here's How:

1. Follow manufacturer's instructions for conditioning and softening polymer clay.
2. Roll clay out like dough to about 1/4 inch thickness.
3. Press rubber stamp designs into clay and trim away clay into a tile shape using a craft knife.
4. Rub gold bronzing powder over the clay pieces using the tip of your finger.
5. Place all clay pieces on cardboard and bake in the oven according to clay manufacturer's directions. Allow tiles to cool.
6. Brush two coats of sealer over tiles, allowing to dry between coats.
7. Brush high-gloss finish on tiles according to manufacturer's instructions. Allow to dry for at least 24 hours.
8. Glue these tiles onto mosaic project 🙰

PRETTY PIECES WINDOW BOX

Created By Connie Sheerin

This window box adds a touch of cheerfulness and playfulness to your indoor or outdoor garden. The sides are created using the mosaic techniques described throughout this chapter and the end bow designs are made using a new technique. Follow these instructions to learn a new technique for enhancing your mosaic designs.

SUPPLIES NEEDED

Project surface:
   Wooden planter, 10-1/2" x 6-1/2" x 5"

For preparing wood:
   Sandpaper
   Wood primer
   Acrylic craft paints: light yellow,
      medium blue, and white
   Sponge brush
   Small brush

For making raised design on planter ends:
   Modelling paste
   Rubber spatula or nylon trowel
   Craft foam
   Graphite transfer paper
   Paper & pencil
   Craft knife

For preparing mosaic pieces:
   Old china plates with patterns
   14 - 16 half marbles
   Rubber mallet
   Newspaper or paper bags
   Glass nippers
   Safety glasses

For assembling & finishing:
   All-purpose white glue
   Sand-free tile grout
   Bowl
   Sponge
   Scissors
   Spray sealer

HERE'S HOW

Prepare wood:
1. Lightly sand wood planter. Wipe away dust.
2. Coat planter with primer using a sponge brush. Allow to dry.
3. Paint planter with two coats of white paint, allowing to dry between coats. It is unnecessary to paint long sides of planter which will be covered with mosaic.
4. Paint side trim and ends of planter with medium blue.
5. Paint top of handles and top of side trim with light yellow.

Create raised design on planter ends:
6. Trace pattern supplied here onto tracing paper.
7. Use graphite transfer paper to transfer pattern onto craft foam.
8. Cut design from craft foam using a craft knife, creating a stencil.
9. Place craft foam stencil onto end of planter.
10. Spread modelling paste over the craft foam using rubber spatula or nylon trowel. Make sure the paste fills in all the design cut-outs.
11. Allow paste to dry for 4 - 6 hours and then remove the craft foam from table top.
12. Paint the raised design with white. Use two coats of paint.
13. Retouch blue paint around raised design if necessary.
14. Create raised design for the other side of the planter.
15. Spray entire planter with outdoor sealer.

Prepare mosaic pieces:
16. Place china plates, one at a time, between layers of newspaper or in a paper bag and break with a mallet. Wear safety glasses.
17. Use glass nippers to cut plate pieces smaller (about 1/2 inch - 1 inch pieces) in a variety of shapes.

Plan mosaic design:
18. Trace side of planter onto paper and cut out tracing to use as a template.
19. Place half marbles and mosaic pieces on template, planning the design. Leave 1/8 inch - 1/4 inch space between mosaic pieces. Refer to photo for placement ideas.

Assemble & finish:
20. Glue half marbles and mosaic pieces onto side of planter as they are laid out on template. Allow glue to dry.
21. Prepare grout and apply to sides of planter as explained in general instructions. Allow to dry and wipe off grout according to general instructions.
22. Retouch paint on planter if necessary.
23. Spray planter with two coats of sealer. ✄

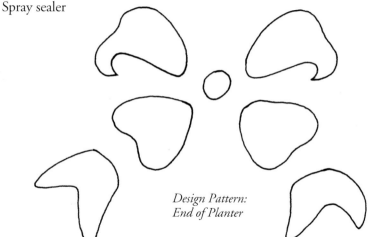

Design Pattern:
End of Planter

CHAPTER 3

OUTDOOR PAINTED ART

Painting fences, furniture, and planters that you use in your garden is not only an enjoyable expression of your creativity, but will also add a delightful decorative element to your outdoor living space. Demonstrate your talent and attention to detail by using furniture that is hand-painted, by you! Or liven an otherwise plain porch or patio with a painted scene. You can use your painting skills to create the look of stones, ponds, and flowers in the areas of your garden that are lacking these natural beauties, such as on the cement walkway or side fence. Painting allows you to add color and creative dimension to the many places and small spaces in your garden that are often taken for granted.

Adding painted art to your outdoor areas is a simple and pleasant activity. First, prepare your surface for painting. If it is wood, preparation may require some sanding. For other surfaces, you usually only need to clean them. Then, plan your design and transfer it onto the project surface, if necessary. Next, you will paint your design, which is often, thanks to the wonderful new decorating products available today, as easy as using a foam stamp or simple stencil. This chapter provides an array of delightful painting project ideas and shows you step-by-step how to paint your outdoor projects.

Birdhouse Village Bench:
See page 54 for project instructions.

PAINTING ON WOOD

SUPPLIES TO USE

PROJECT SURFACES

Any type of wood surface, old or new, makes a wonderful base for your outdoor painting. You can paint on wood **fences, furniture, floors, or decorative items**. Old pieces of wood furniture found at flea markets are perfect candidates for decorative painting. You may also purchase new, unfinished wood pieces for your painting projects.

PAINT

Exterior latex paint works well for covering large areas of your wood pieces. You can even use this type of paint for painting the designs on your pieces.

Acrylic craft paints can be used for more detailed painting. As long as you have a good sealer on top of them, they can withstand the weather. You will also be able to find acrylic craft paints that are especially developed for outdoor use. Either type can be used for decorative painting.

Stencil paints and **colored glazes** are also appropriate for outdoor use when either stenciling or stamping your project. Again a good outdoor sealer on top of the paint will make it suitable for outdoor use.

BRUSHES

Paint brushes come in a variety of shapes, sizes, and quality. Both synthetic bristle and natural bristle brushes are available. However, **synthetic brushes** will work well enough for decorative painting. Buy the best quality brushes that you can afford. Also buy brushes with the right shape for the task at hand. Round, flat, and stencil brushes all work very differently. Brushes work best when you are using the correct shape as well as the largest size that you can use in the space available. You can use **sponge brushes** when applying a basecoat, primer, or sealer and you can use a **paint roller** when covering a large area with exterior latex paint.

PRIMERS & SEALERS

A good quality **exterior wood primer** will seal your wood project and make it easier to paint. It provides bonding agents between the wood surface and the first layer of paint. After you have painted your project, you will need to protect it from the weather. Use either a **spray or brush-on sealer** that is made for outdoor use.

STENCIL & FOAM STAMPS

Several of the projects in this chapter use modern decorative products for simple, beautiful, professional-looking painting.

For stenciling projects, you will need a **pre-cut stencil, stencil brushes, and stencil paint**. Stencils are available for sale at craft and art stores. You can also make your own stencils by using a **marker** to trace a design onto **acetate** or **blank stencil material** and then cutting the design out with a **craft knife**.

Foam stamps are a wonderful way to create a design that is neat and quick like stenciling, but more random and natural. Foam stamps come in many design shapes and are available at craft stores. Foam stamping is sometimes referred to as block-printing. For stamping, you will need to use a special **colored gel-glaze**, also available at craft stores. Acrylic craft paint will also give good results with stamping.

TOOLS NEEDED

Graphite transfer paper, a pencil, and tracing paper are used for transferring the design to the project surface.

Sandpaper and a rag are used for preparing the wood surface.

Sponges are used for applying paint on some projects.

A ruler and masking tape are used for marking off straight lines for painting and also for planning design placement.

HERE'S HOW

Prepare surface:
1. Sand unfinished wood with medium grit sandpaper followed by a fine grit sandpaper, sanding in the direction of the grain. *NOTE: If wood is already painted or finished, remove paint with a sanding block and 80 grit paper. After paint is removed, continue sanding as unfinished wood.*
2. Remove dust with a rag or tack cloth.
3. Use a sponge brush to apply exterior primer to wood following manufacturer's instructions. Allow to dry.
4. Sand surface with #200, then #400 grit sandpaper to smooth the primer.
5. Remove dust.
6. Basecoat project surface if necessary by applying two coats of paint. Allow paint to dry and sand between coats.

Plan and transfer design:
7. Plan the placement of the design, referring to the photo. For some designs, you can paint them free-hand.

Continued on next page

Another option is to sketch the design free-hand with a pencil before painting.

8. For more detailed designs, you may wish to transfer the design using graphite transfer paper. First, enlarge the pattern given in this book with a copy machine and then transfer the enlarged design. *NOTE: You can also enlarge the pattern by creating a grid on the pattern and an enlarged grid on your project surface. Then, sketch the design onto the project surface, drawing each grid section one at a time. For example, if the pattern needs to be enlarged four times, you should use a ruler to draw 1 inch squares on the pattern and 4 inch squares on the project surface. Then draw on the surface exactly what you see on each square of your grid design.*

Paint design:

9. Follow individual project instructions for painting and decorating instructions. Remember while painting to use the largest brush possible for the area being painted. Most projects in this book use acrylic craft paint for painting design details.

Finish:

10. After all paint has dried, you should seal your project for protection against the weather and use. Apply at least two coats of either a spray or brush-on sealer that is made for outdoor use. Follow manufacturer's instructions. ❦

GENERAL PAINTING TECHNIQUES

Painting With Acrylics

Acrylic Craft Paints are a wonderful choice for decorative painting on most any surface. All the design painting shown in this book have been painted with acrylic craft paints. There are a variety of brands on the market, each offering a rainbow of colors. When working with acrylics be sure to properly prepare your surface, then adequately seal when painting is complete for outside use. You may also be able to find acrylic craft enamels that are especially formulated for outdoor use. There paints are more fade and weather resistant. Following are some tips when painting with acrylics.

- Squeeze paint from bottle to your palette, making a puddle of paint about the size of a nickel.
- Don't dip your brush into your puddle of paint, *Pull* it with your brush from the edge of the paint puddle. Dipping puts too much paint on the edge of your brush.
- Let each coat dry before applying a second coat. To check dryness, touch the surface. If an area is cool to the touch, it is probably still wet. Work on another area of your project while one area is drying.
- Acrylic paints blend easily. Add white to lighten a color. Add black to darken.

Brush Care

Your brush is the most important tool used in painting. Care of these brushes is a must. Use a good water container to rinse brushes. Change the water often. Never leave your brushes standing in water. Clean them at the end of the day with brush cleaner. Store them bristle-side-up in a tall container or brush carrier.

Using the Patterns Given

Because we want to offer you as much information and as many designs as possible, we have chosen to give you SOME of the painting patterns at a smaller size than actual size. When this is the case, we have indicated at what percent to enlarge the pattern to make it the actual size shown on our projects. Photo copy machines are so prevalent today, that it is quite easy to have your pattern enlarged for a nominal fee. Most libraries and quick print shops offer this service.

TRACING PATTERNS:

1. If the pattern in this book is actual size, place a sheet of tracing paper over the pattern and trace the main lines of the pattern with a pencil or permanent marker. If you have a photo copy of your pattern, do not do this step.
2. Position traced design or photo copied pattern onto project surface. Secure with tape. Slip a piece of transfer paper (white or black is available), velvet side down, between the pattern and the project surface. Use a stylus or ball point pen to retrace the pattern lines, using enough pressure to transfer the lines but not so much that you indent the surface.

PAINTING ON CEMENT

SUPPLIES TO USE

PROJECT SURFACES

Any type of cement surface, old or new, makes a wonderful base for your outdoor painting. You can paint on cement **patios, furniture, or decorative items such as birdbaths and statues**. You may purchase new cement pieces for your painting projects or decorate the cement areas around your garden.

PAINT

Waterproof primer will be needed as a first coat sealer. Concrete is very porous and a primer is needed to keep it from soaking up water and causing paint to bubble.

Exterior cement paint is needed for basecoating your cement projects. Some cement paints may also contain a waterproof sealer.

You may also use **acrylic craft paints** for painting more detailed designs on top of your basecoated surface.

BRUSHES

FOR BASECOATING the cement, an inexpensive **foam brush or synthetic bristle wall paint brushes** will be fine. If you are basecoating a large flat surface such as a patio floor, **paint rollers** will be more convenient to use.

FOR DESIGN PAINTING, you will need to use **artist brushes**. Artist brushes come in a variety of shapes, sizes, and quality. Both synthetic bristle and natural bristle brushes are available. However, synthetic brushes will work well enough for decorative painting on cement since the roughness of the cement will be hard on your brushes. Buy brushes with the right shape for the task at hand. Round, flat, and stencil brushes all work very differently. Brushes work best when you are using the correct shape as well as the largest size that you can use in the space available.

CLEANERS

Cleaning the cement surface of your project is very important. Be sure to remove all dirt and grease. Use a **dust cloth, broom, or brush** to remove dust and dirt. Small pieces of ornamental concrete can be cleaned using an **old paint brush** and **rubbing alcohol**. Use **muriatic acid** mixed with water to clean grease from large concrete surfaces. If using muriatic acid, you will also need **protective glasses and rubber gloves.**

STENCILS

Stencils are a wonderful tool for simple, beautiful, professional-looking painting. For stenciling projects, you will need **a stencil and stencil brushes.** Concrete paint can be used as stencil paint. Stencils are available for sale at craft and art stores. You can also make your own stencils by using a **marker** to trace a design onto **acetate** or **blank stencil material** and then cutting the design out with a **craft knife.**

SEALERS

After your design painting is complete, use a clear outdoor finish to protect your painting.

TOOLS NEEDED

Graphite transfer paper, a pencil, and tracing paper are used for transferring the design to the project surface.

Sponges are used for applying paint on some projects.

A ruler and masking tape are used for marking off straight lines for painting and also for planning design placement.

HERE'S HOW

Prepare surface:

1. Clean dust and dirt off cement surface with water and a brush or cloth. For large areas, dip broom into water to scrub the surface. After scrubbing, hose off the dirt. Allow cement to dry.
2. If necessary, clean grease off cement surface. For small pieces of ornamental cement, use an old paint brush and rubbing alcohol to scrub off grease. For large cement areas, use a mixture of muriatic acid and water with an old broom to clean off grease. Follow manufacturer's directions. Wear protective glasses and rubber gloves.

NOTE: Avoid getting muriatic acid solution on plants. If you do, water plants well to dissolve solution.

3. Rinse off cleaners with water, using a hose for large cement areas. Allow cement to dry **thoroughly.**
4. Apply primer and allow to dry.
5. Basecoat surface with cement paint and allow to dry.

Plan and transfer design:

6. Plan the placement of the design, referring to the photo.

Continued on next page

For some designs, you can paint them free-hand. Another option is to sketch the design free-hand with a pencil before painting.

7. For more detailed designs, you may wish to transfer the design using graphite transfer paper. First, enlarge your design with a copy machine and then transfer the enlarged design. *NOTE: You can also enlarge the pattern by creating a grid on the pattern and an enlarged grid on your project surface. Then, sketch the design onto the project surface, drawing each grid section one at a time. For example, if the pattern needs to be enlarged four times, you should use a ruler to draw 1 inch squares on the pattern and 4 inch squares on the project surface. Then draw on surface exactly what you see on each sqare of grid.*

Paint design:

8. Follow individual project instructions for painting and decorating instructions. Remember while painting to use the largest brush possible for the area being painted.

Finish:

9. Allow concrete paint to dry for at least 24 hours. It may need up to 48 hours to dry thoroughly.

10. Apply a good quality outdoor sealer or finish. Several coats will be necessary. ❦

Painting Terms

Loading Your Brush: Pull the side of your brush along the edge of the paint puddle to load it with paint. Do not dip it into paint. Wipe your brush back and forth on your palette in one spot to distribute the paint through the brush.

Double Loading Brush: With this technique you will be loading two colors of paint onto one flat brush. Dampen brush with water or medium and touch on a paper towel to absorb excess liquid. Flatten the brush on the palette. Pull one side edge of the brush through the edge of the paint puddle. Pull the other side (clean side) of the flattened brush through a second paint color. Blend your brush back and forth on one spot of the palette. The colors should begin to blend in the center of the brush and be distinct on each side.

Side Loading: Loading one color onto a corner of a brush that has been moistened with water or medium.

Floating: Moisten a flat brush with water or medium. Touch brush to paper towel to absorb excess moisture. Load one side edge of the brush. Blend brush well in one spot on your palette. Use this method for highlighting or shading areas.

Basecoating: To basecoat is to simply fill in an area of the design (or the background) with a solid coat of color. Paint with as few strokes as possible to eliminate brush strokes.

Undercoating: When painting with light colors on a dark surface, you may need to undercoat a part of the design with white paint in order for your design paint color to show.

Shading: Shading creates shadows, darkens and deepens color, and makes an area recede. In decorative painting, one side of an object is often shaded to add depth and dimension. To shade, dampen brush with water or a painting medium. Load shading color of paint on only one side of a flat brush. Paint shadowed area, applying paint in a "floating" technique.

Highlighting: Highlighting adds dimension by adding light in the form of a lighter color. It also makes an area seem closer. Highlight with a lighter color, using the same "floating" technique as used for shading.

Pouncing: Use an old beat-up flat brush to add irregular dots of color to your project by bouncing the bristles with paint up and down in an area. Pouncing can also be accomplished with a stencil brush, deerfoot brush, or sponge.

Drybrush: This technique is usually used to add a hint of color. Let your painting dry. Do not pick up painting medium in your brush. Pick up color on a flat brush and wipe it almost free of paint. You will be surprised how much color remains. Apply to painting surface with quick crosshatch strokes.

Spattering: Spattering gives a speckled effect. It adds an interesting finishing touch. Test your spattering on a piece of paper before applying it to project. Cover your work space, place project in a box, or work outdoors to avoid paint spatters where you don't want them. Dip a stencil brush or toothbrush in water. Blot. Mix paint with water until it has the consistency of ink. Pick up paint color on brush. Hold brush 12" from your project. Pull a palette knife across the bristles to release the paint and splatter it onto surface. Move around the project, continuing until the results please you.

Scruffy Brush: An old, beat-up flat brush with splayed bristles. This type of brush is good for pouncing or stippling. ❦

PAINTING ON METAL

SUPPLIES TO USE

PROJECT SURFACES

A wonderful variety of metal surfaces can be used for decorating your garden with outdoor painting. You can paint on aluminum, iron, steel, solid brass, bronze, copper or plated brass. Metal **fences, furniture, or decorative items** are all perfect candidates for decorative painting. You may purchase new metal pieces for your painting projects or rejuvenate old pieces found at flea markets or your very own garage or attic.

PAINT

Exterior acrylic paint works well for covering metal pieces. For detailed painting, you can use **acrylic craft paints.**

BRUSHES

FOR BASECOATING the metal, an inexpensive **foam brush or synthetic bristle wall paint brushes** will be fine. If you are basecoating a large flat surface, a **paint roller** will be more convenient to use. These types of brushes can also be used for applying the sealer and finish.

FOR DESIGN PAINTING, you will need to use **artist brushes.** Artist brushes come in a variety of shapes, sizes, and quality. Both synthetic bristle and natural bristle brushes are available. However, synthetic brushes will work well enough for decorative painting on metal. Buy brushes with the right shape for the task at hand. Round, flat, and stencil brushes all work very differently. Brushes work best when you are using the correct shape as well as the largest size that you can use in the space available.

CLEANERS

If your metal surface has a lacquered finish, this will need to be removed before painting. Use **0000 steel wool and denatured alcohol**. Wear **rubber gloves and protective glasses**. When painting an older metal piece, you may need to remove rust with a **wire brush and sandpaper**. Brass, copper, and silver should be cleaned with **tarnish remover** before painting.

PRIMERS & SEALERS

A good quality **rust inhibitive oil base primer** should be applied to your metal surface before painting. After you have painted your project, you will need to protect it from the weather. Use either a **spray or brush-on sealer** that is made for outdoor use.

STENCILS

Stencils are a wonderful tool for simple, beautiful, professional-looking painting. For stenciling projects, you will need **a stencil and stencil brushes.** Stencils are available for sale at craft and art stores. You can also make your own stencils by using a **marker** to trace a design onto **acetate** or **blank stencil material** and then cutting the design out with a **craft knife.**

TOOLS NEEDED

Graphite transfer paper, chalk, a pencil, and tracing paper are used for transferring the design to the project surface.

Sponges are used for applying paint on some projects.

A ruler and masking tape are used for marking off straight lines for painting and also for planning design placement.

HERE'S HOW

Prepare surface:

1. Determine if the surface has a lacquered finish by running the edge of a razor blade over the surface. If small translucent flakes fall off, the surface has a lacquered finish that must be removed before painting.
2. If necessary, remove lacquer coating by using a piece of #0000 steel wool dipped in denatured alcohol. Clean the surface with cloth and denatured alcohol. Wear rubber gloves and protective glasses. Also be sure to work in a well-ventilated area.
3. Remove rust or flaking paint from surface with a wire brush. Use metal sandpaper to further remove rust and smooth metal surface.
4. Use a tarnish remover to clean brass, copper, or silver before painting.
5. Apply two coats of rust inhibitive oil base primer to metal surface. This is available in spray cans or paint containers. If painting on, use inexpensive sponge brushes to apply. Allow primer to dry according to manufacturer's directions.

Continued on next page

Plan and transfer design:

6. Plan the placement of the design, referring to the photo. For some designs, you can paint them free-hand. Another option is to sketch the design free-hand with chalk before painting.

7. For more detailed designs, you may wish to transfer the design using graphite transfer paper. First, enlarge the pattern given in this book with a copy machine and then transfer the enlarged design.

Paint design:

8. Follow individual project instructions for painting and decorating instructions. Remember while painting to use the largest brush possible for the area being painted.

Finish:

9. After all paint has dried, you should seal your project for protection against the weather and use. Apply at least two coats of either a spray or brush-on sealer that is made for outdoor use. Follow manufacturer's instructions. 🐝

Southern Dogwood Watering Can, see page 60.

TROMPE L'OEIL PAINTED FENCE
Created By Kathi Malarchuk

This design is a beautiful way to add depth, dimension, and color to a plain wooden fence. You could paint a section of your surrounding fence, or just paint this on a small piece of fence to be used as a divider between different areas of your garden. The design is fun and very easy to paint since stencils and foam stamps will help you to create the pots and foliage.

SUPPLIES NEEDED

Project surface:
Wood fence panel

Paint:
Exterior latex paint, white, satin or eggshell finish for basecoating fence
Exterior latex paint for color washes, 1 pint each: shrimp colored, sage, medium blue
Colored glaze paint for design stamping, 2 oz.: sage, deep woods green, ivy green, rose, brown
Stencil paint: russet, pumpkin, twig, taupe, black
Neutral glazing medium, 48 oz.

Brushes:
Sponge brush
Stencil brushes
Flat brush
Round brush

Primers & sealers:
Wood primer
Outdoor sealer

Stencils & foam stamps:
Leaf variety foam stamps
Cut-your-own foam material
Pots & planters stencil

Tools:
Sandpaper
Paint roller
Sea sponge
Masking tape
Palette or disposable plates
Brush basin
Blank paper
White charcoal pencil
Black marker
Craft knife
Tape measure
Pencil

Closeup of fence design.

Instructions continued on pages 40 & 41

Here's How— Trompe l'oeil Painted Fence

Prepare wood:

1. Sand wood, wipe away dust, apply primer, and sand again following general instructions for painting on wood.

2. Use paint roller to basecoat fence with two coats of white exterior latex paint, allowing to dry and sanding between coats. Allow paint to dry before continuing.

3. Mix shrimp colored latex paint with glazing medium in a 1:1 ratio. Wet sea sponge and wring out excess water until damp. Dip into shrimp colored glaze and wipe over lower third of fence panel. Clean sponge.

4. Mix sage colored latex paint with glazing medium in a 1:1 ratio. Use damp sponge to wipe sage colored glaze over middle third section of fence. Blend glaze where two colors meet. Clean sponge.

5. Mix medium blue latex paint with glazing medium in a 1:1 ratio. Use damp sponge to wipe blue colored glaze over top third section of fence. Blend glaze where colors meet. Clean sponge.

6. Lightly dab over joined areas with a damp clean sponge to blend colors thoroughly. Allow to dry 24 hours.

Stencil table and pots:

7. Using the pattern given, measure and draw onto fence, the table section of design. Mark with light pencil marks.

8. Use masking tape to tape off table and leg sections according to pattern given. Complete one section at a time so that tape does not overlap.

9. Pour equal amounts of twig, russet, and black stencil paint onto palette. Blend twig and russet. Refer to photo #1.

10. Load stencil brush with blended color by rubbing it into the paint. Blot off excess paint on a clean section of the plate. Refer to photo #2.

11. Stencil table area using masking tape as stencil. Shade table with black stencil paint.

12. Attach pot stencil to fence above table with masking tape, following photo on page 38 for placement. Refer to photo #3.

13. Pour equal amounts of russet, pumpkin, and twig stencil paint onto palette.

14. Blend russet and pumpkin to a terra cotta color and load stencil brush.

15. Stencil large and small pots with terra cotta color. Begin stenciling by swirling paint on an uncut portion of the stencil and moving into the stencil opening, continuing to swirl brush. Continue until you have stenciled entire opening. Refer to photo #3.

16. Shade pots with twig stencil paint. Refer to photo #4.

17. Create rim on pots by lowering top of pot stencil to just under outer rim and shade lower section with twig. Refer to photo #5.

18. Pour equal amounts of taupe, twig, and black stencil paint onto palette.

19. Stencil stone pot on lower left side with a blend of taupe and twig. Shade with black.

Stamp foliage:

20. To create hand cut leaves, transfer leaf pattern given onto blank paper with black marker. Turn paper over and trace back of pattern with white charcoal pencil. Press onto cut-your-own foam material. Use craft knife to cut the stamp form, following manufacturer's instructions.

21. Load handcut stamps with deep woods green and ivy green colored gel glaze by painting the surface of the stamps using a brush loaded with colored glaze. Refer to photo #6.

22. Press loaded stamp onto fence to create ivy on pots, referring to photo for placement ideas. Refer to photo #7.

23. Lift stamp to reveal leaf shape. Refer to photo #8.

24. Load round brush with ivy green colored glaze to paint ivy stems directly onto fence.

25. Load long leaves from leaf variety foam stamps with ivy green and brown colored glaze.

26. Stamp leaves onto willow tree, stopping at approximately 54 inches from the bottom of fence. Refer to photo for placement ideas.

27. Load flat brush with brown colored glaze to paint trunk, stems, and branches on willow tree.

28. Load oval leaves from leaf variety foam stamps with ivy green and deep woods green colored glaze.

29. Stamp leaves on center pots on table to create foliage for cone flowers.

Paint cone flowers:

30. Load round brush with rose and taupe colored glaze to paint cone flower petals. Lay tip of brush down, pull brush down, and lift to create tear drop shapes.

31. Dip round brush in brown colored glaze to stipple center onto flowers.

32. Load round brush with ivy green colored glaze to paint stems on flowers.

Finish design:

33. Dip stencil brush in ivy green and brown colored glaze to stipple moss and dirt on sides of pots.

34. Allow fence to dry 48 hours.

35. Brush or spray on outdoor sealer according to general instructions for painting wood. ❧

Trompe l'oeil Painted Fence
Painting Pattern

72"

54"

12-1/2"

9-1/2"

2"

1"

24"

21"

2"

1"

35"

1"

17"

3"

42"

42

Cut-Your-Own Leaves Pattern

Transfer patterns onto cut-your-own foam material and cut out with a craft knife.

FAUX STONE PATIO FLOOR
Created By Kathi Malarchuk

Change a simple cement patio into a beautiful cobblestone patio with some well-placed paint! This design is quick, easy, and can be adapted to cover as large or small an area as you desire.

SUPPLIES NEEDED

Project Surface:
Cement patio
Waterproof cement primer or sealer

Paint:
Exterior cement paint, sandstone, 1 gallon for basecoating floor
Exterior latex paint for stenciling stone design: parchment, terra cotta, brown, dark gray

Stencil:
Cut-your-own stencil material or 18 inches x 1 yard blank acetate

Tools:
Paint rollers, large and small
4 sea sponges
Palette or disposable plates
Blank paper
Black marker
Craft knife
Cutting surface, such as glass or rotary mat
Broom or scrub brush & muriatic acid for cleaning cement, if necessary
Safety glasses & rubber gloves, if using muriatic acid

Instructions continued on pages 46 & 47

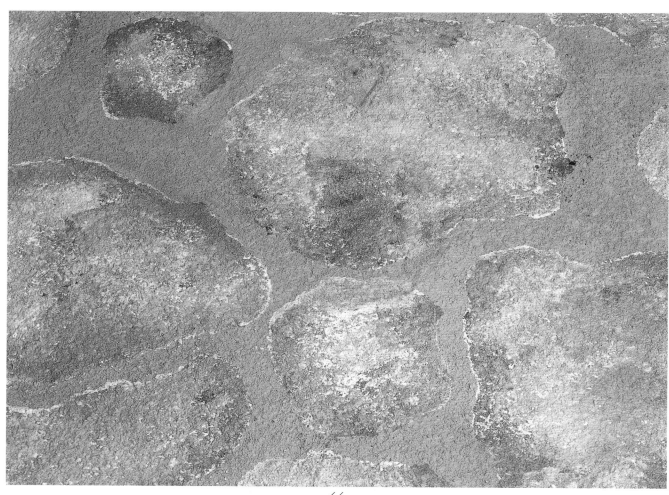

HERE'S HOW — FAUX STONE PATIO FLOOR

Prepare surface:

1. Clean dust, dirt, and grease off cement surface. Rinse off cleaners and allow cement to dry. Apply primer. Refer to general instructions for painting cement.
2. Apply two coats of sandstone cement paint using a paint roller over entire patio. Allow to dry for 24 hours.

Create stencil:

3. Transfer cobblestone patterns provided here onto blank paper with a marker.
4. Lay acetate or blank stencil material over traced pattern and use marker to trace pattern again. Refer to photo #1.
5. Lay acetate or blank stencil material on a cutting surface and use a craft knife to cut out cobblestone shapes from acetate or blank stencil material. Refer to photo #2.

1

2

3

4

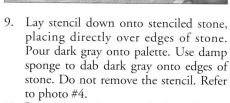

5

Stencil design:

6. Pour parchment paint onto palette and load small roller with paint.
7. Lay stencil onto patio and use the roller to fill shape. Refer to photo #3.
8. Lift stencil and move stencil. Stencil a parchment colored stone in this area of patio. Continue to fill the patio area with stenciled stones, varying the size and position of the stones. Leave 1/4 inch to 1/2 inch between stones. Allow to dry.

9. Lay stencil down onto stenciled stone, placing directly over edges of stone. Pour dark gray onto palette. Use damp sponge to dab dark gray onto edges of stone. Do not remove the stencil. Refer to photo #4.
10. Repeat sponging around edge of stone using terra cotta paint. Refer to photo #5.
11. Mix parchment and brown in a 1 to 1 ratio and use to continue sponging edge of stone.

12. Place stencil on the next stone and sponge the edges with dark gray, terra cotta, and parchment/brown mix.
13. Continue sponging the edges of all stones on patio.

Finish:

14. Allow concrete paint to dry for at least 24 hours. It may need up to 48 hours to dry thoroughly.
15. Apply sealer. 🐝

Stencil Patterns for Stones

Transfer patterns onto cut-your-own stencil material and cut out with a craft knife.
For size shown in photo, enlarge on copy machine @135%.

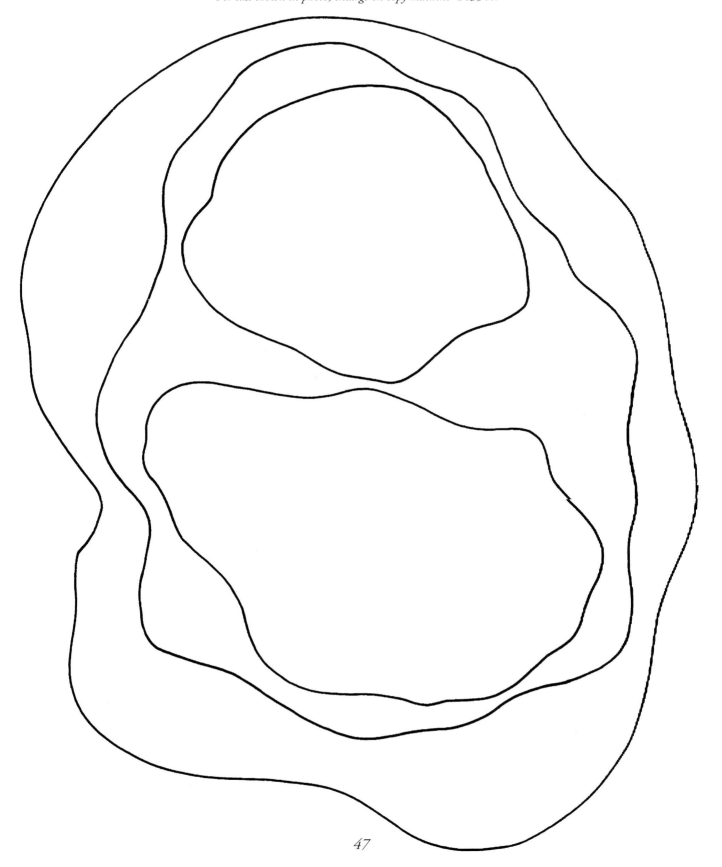

IVY PRIVACY

Created By Kathi Malarchuk

This design is wonderfully adaptable to any size surface you wish to decorate. Here we show a fence divider that is the perfect way to hide garbage cans.

SUPPLIES NEEDED

Project surface:
Wood fence panel

Paint:
Exterior latex paint, white, satin or eggshell finish for basecoating fence
Colored glaze, 2 oz.: deep woods green, ivy green, new leaf green, bark brown

Brushes:
Sponge brush
Flat brush
#5 round brush

Primers & sealers:
Outdoor sealer

Foam stamps:
Leaf variety foam stamps

Tools:
Sandpaper
Paint roller
Palette or disposable plates
Brush basin

Optional, for hanging pot holders:
Wrought iron flower pot holders
Wood screws
Screwdriver

HERE'S HOW

Prepare wood:
1. Sand wood, wipe away dust.
2. Use paint roller to apply one thin coat of paint to fence using white exterior latex paint. Allow to dry then sand lightly. This will create a washed and worn look to fence.

Paint design:
3. Use a flat brush to brush new leaf green colored glaze onto a large leaf stamp.
4. Press stamp onto fence, referring to photo for placement ideas.
5. Continuing stamping design on fence. Load large and small round leaf stamps with new leaf green and ivy green colored glazes. Add deep woods green glaze to edges of stamps for shading.
6. Load round brush with bark brown and ivy green colored glaze to add branches and stems on ivy.

Finish:
7. Allow to dry 48 hours.
8. Brush or spray on outdoor sealer according to general instructions for painting wood.
9. Attach flower pot holders to fence with screws. ❦

POND AT YOUR FOOTSTEPS

Created By
Bunny Delorie

Paint this design on your cement stoop leading out to the garden as a perfect way to bridge the space between indoor and outdoor. This stoop is adjacent to a screened porch.

Instructions on pages 52 & 53

POND AT YOUR FOOTSTEPS

SUPPLIES NEEDED

Project surface:
Cement patio or porch floor

Paint:
Exterior cement paint, sandstone
Acrylic craft paint: umber, sand, medium gray, yellow ochre, leaf green, deep sea green, burgundy, black, ivory, moss green, yellow green, light teal, rust
Glazing medium, 1/4 quart

Brushes:
Large stippling brush, 1-1/2" - 2" diameter
Flat brush
Round brush
Liner brush
Sponge brushes, 1/2", 1", and 2"

Sealer:
Outdoor sealer

Tools:
Paint roller
3 sea sponges
Palette or disposable plates
3 plastic containers, 1 quart
Broom or brush & muriatic acid for cleaning cement, if necessary
Safety glasses & rubber gloves if using muriatic acid

Painting Pattern — Actual Size

HERE'S HOW

Prepare surface:

1. Clean dust, dirt, and grease off cement surface. Rinse off cleaners and allow cement to dry. Refer to general instructions for sealing and painting cement.
2. Apply two coats of sandstone cement paint using a paint roller over entire surface to be painted. Allow to dry for 24 hours.

Transfer design:

3. Transfer design onto surface according to general instructions for painting on cement.

Paint pond design:

4. Load sponge brush with light teal to basecoat pond. Do not paint lily pads. Allow to dry.
5. In a plastic container, thoroughly mix 1 oz. glazing medium with 1 oz. deep sea green paint.
6. Pour a small amount of black paint onto palette.
7. Wet sponge and wring out excess water. Dip damp sponge into glaze mixture and blot onto palette.
8. Beginning at left side of pond, sponge glaze onto pond, applying to a small area at a time.
9. As more glaze is applied, start introducing some black paint as you progress across to right side of pond and around pond edges. Dip sponge into glaze, then dip one corner into black paint.
10. Load flat brush with glaze to fill in pond edges.
11. While glaze is wet, pounce area with stippling brush to soften and remove any obvious sponge marks.

Paint grout around stones:

12. Pour small amounts of umber, sand, ivory, medium gray, yellow ochre, and moss green onto palette.
13. Dip a 1/2" or 1" flat brush into sand color to paint grout lines around stones. Add a small amount of umber to brush, applying paint to grout to shade. Allow to dry.

Paint stones:

14. Wet three sea sponges and wring out excess water.
15. Dip one sponge into sand color and sponge color onto stones.
16. Fill edges of stone with round brush using sand color.
17. Continue sponging stones using medium gray, ivory, and yellow. Rinse sponges as they become muddy.
18. Blend colors with clean side of sponge.
19. Load liner brush with a mixture of umber and medium gray to add shadows and detail to edges of stones.

Paint lily pads:

20. Pour small amounts of leaf green, yellow green, burgundy, and ivory onto palette.
21. Load small flat brush with yellow green to basecoat lily pads. Allow to dry.
22. Mix a 1 to 1 ratio of small amounts of leaf green and glazing medium in a plastic container.
23. Dip flat brush into glaze mixture to float over lily pads.
24. While glaze is wet, load a round brush with leaf green and a

Continued on next page

Continued from page 52

small amount of burgundy. Outline edges of lily pads, blending colors into glaze.
25. Highlight edges of leaves with yellow green. Allow to dry.
26. Load a flat brush with ivory and blot onto paper towel.
27. Use dry brush to highlight lily pads with ivory.
28. Use dry brush technique with burgundy to accent center of lily pads.

Paint turtle:
29. Pour small amounts of umber, sand, medium gray, rust, black, and ivory onto palette.
30. Load round brush with a mixture of umber and sand to paint turtle head and flippers.
31. Add shadows of umber mixed with a small amount of medium grey.
32. Use smaller round brush or a liner brush to paint ivory highlights along flipper edges and detail on head.

33. Load liner brush with a mixture of black and a small amount of umber to paint detail of skin on back flippers.
34. Paint shell in small sections. Brush rust and umber onto each section.
35. Add a small amount of burgundy mixed with umber to outside edges of sections.
36. Add black to paint mixtures as you paint sections on left side of shell.
37. Use liner brush to outline each section on shell with ivory.

Finish:
38. Allow paint to dry for at least 24 hours. It may need up to 48 hours to dry thoroughly.
39. You may wish to apply a sealer to protect your painting from the elements. Use an outdoor spray or brush-on sealer. Follow manufacturer's instructions. 🐝

Design Pattern for Painting

Enlarge on copy machine to fit area on floor.

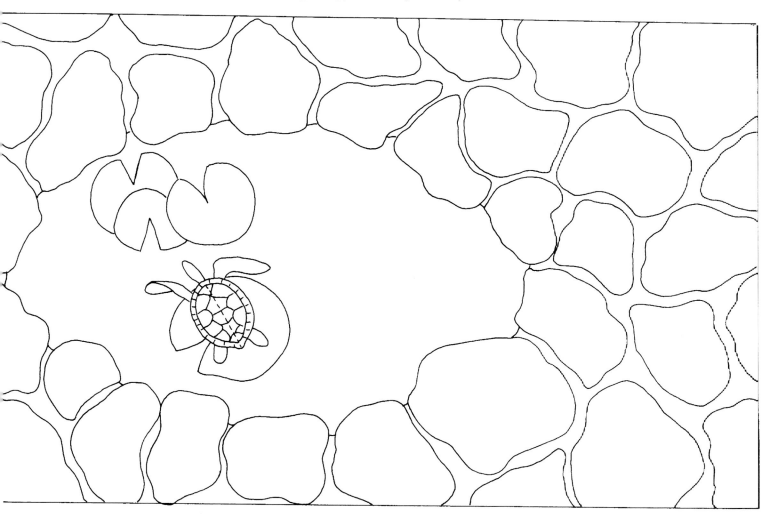

BIRDHOUSE VILLAGE BENCH

CREATED BY JEFF MCWILLIAMS

This elegant white bench is the perfect compliment to a colorful garden. Building your own bench will bring you pride and satisfaction each time you notice its delightful presence in your garden.

SUPPLIES NEEDED

Project surface:
1" x 6" white pine
1" x 3" white pine
1/4" plywood
1-1/8" x 1/4" molding or 1/4" plywood

Paint:
Exterior latex paint, white, satin or eggshell finish

Brushes:
Sponge brush
Large paint brush

Primer:
Wood primer

Tools:
Sandpaper, medium and fine
1-1/2" drill bit and drill
Scroll saw
Wood glue
Tape measure
Pencil
Wood putty
Nail set
6d finishing nails
Wood screws: four 1/4" x 3", 60, 1/8" x 1-1/4"

HERE'S HOW

Assemble seat frame:
1. Cut frame pieces from 1" x 3" stock:
   front piece 45-3/4" long
   back piece 44-1/4" long
   2 ends 16-1/4" long
   2 braces 10-1/2" long
2. Follow assembly diagram and attach ends to front using glue and 6d finishing nails.
3. Attach back and braces similarly.

Assemble bench seat:
1. Cut seat pieces from 1" x 6" stock: 2 pieces 45-3/4" long.
2. Attach seat pieces to frame beginning with the front piece flush with the frame front piece. Leave 1/4" space between the two seat pieces and attach with 6d finishing nails and glue.

Assemble bench sides:
1. Cut side pieces from 1" x 6" stock: 6 pieces 26" long.
2. Cut a "V" notch in the ends of two of the side pieces.
3. Attach 3 side pieces to each end of the frame so that the top of the seat is 16-1/2" from the bottom of the side pieces. Leave 1/4" space between pieces and be sure the notch is in the middle of both ends. Use glue and wood screws (from the inside) to attach.
4. Cut arm rests from 1" stock: 2 pieces 2-1/2" x 19".
5. Attach arm rests flush with inside edge of bench sides using glue and 6d finishing nails. Rests extend 1" beyond side pieces front and back.

Assemble bench back:
1. Cut back pieces from 1" x 6" stock: 8 pieces at various lengths described in diagram. Cut 2 braces from 1" x 3" stock, 45-3/4" long.
2. Attach braces to back sides of back pieces using wood screws and glue (see diagram).
3. Attach back to seat so that bottom edge rests on seat frame. Angle back at slope of 1-1/2" in 10" and attach with 3" wood screws through end boards into the brace for the back boards. Also screw and glue bottom of back boards to seat.

Add details:
1. Cut roof pieces from 1-1/8" x 1/4" molding or use 1/4" plywood. Measure lengths needed directly from the back boards. Attach with glue to the face of the back pieces as shown by the shading on the diagram.
2. Drill 1-1/2" diameter holes through back boards where indicated on diagram.
3. Cut 2-1/4" square as shown on diagram rounding out the corners at the top of the opening.
4. Set all nails and fill holes with wood putty.

Prepare wood for painting:
1. Sand wood, wipe away dust, apply primer, and sand again following general instructions for painting on wood.
2. Use a large paint brush to paint entire bench with two coats of white exterior latex paint, allowing to dry and sanding between coats. Allow paint to dry thoroughly.

Finish:
When paint has dried, use medium sandpaper to sand off the edges of the upright back pieces and remove the edges of the housetops as well. This will create a weather-worn look. Refer to photo. ❧

See page 30 & 31 for a closer view of bench.

Construction Diagrams — Birdhouse Village Bench

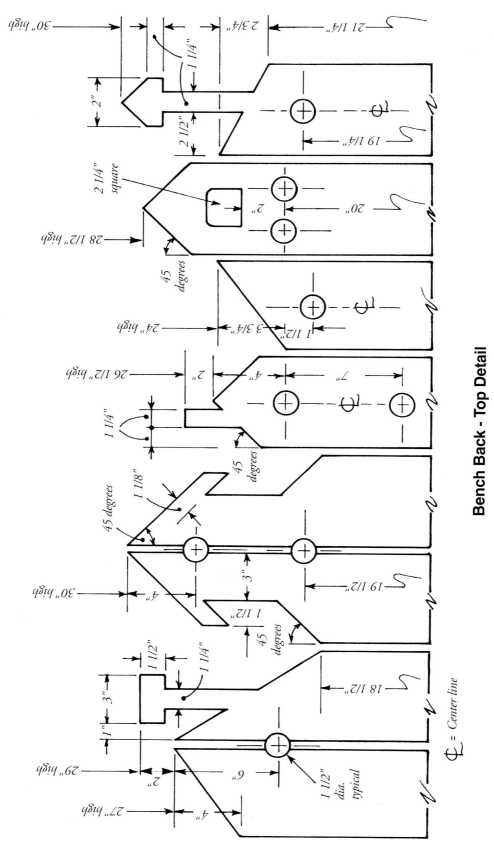

Bench Back - Top Detail

30" high

21 1/4"

2 3/4"

1 1/4"

2"

2 1/2"

19 1/4"

2 1/4" square

28 1/2" high

45 degrees

20"

2"

24" high

3 3/4"

1 1/2"

26 1/2" high

2"

4"

7"

1 1/4"

45 degrees

1 1/8"

45 degrees

3"

1 1/2"

45 degrees

30" high

4"

19 1/2"

1 1/2"

1 1/4"

3"

1"

18 1/2"

29" high

2"

6"

1 1/2" dia. typical

27" high

4"

Ⱡ = Center line

56

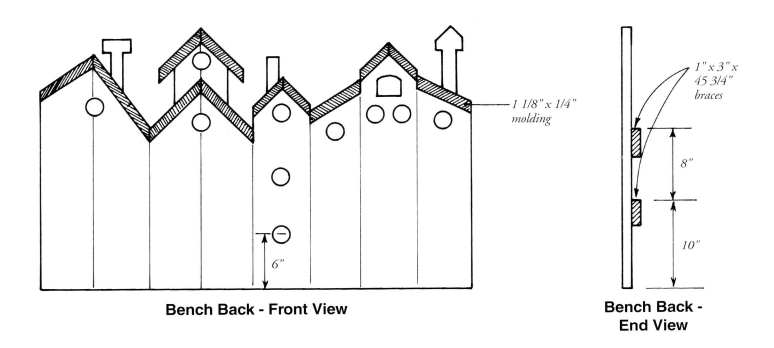

Bench Back - Front View

1 1/8" x 1/4"
molding

**Bench Back -
End View**

1" x 3" x
45 3/4"
braces

8"

10"

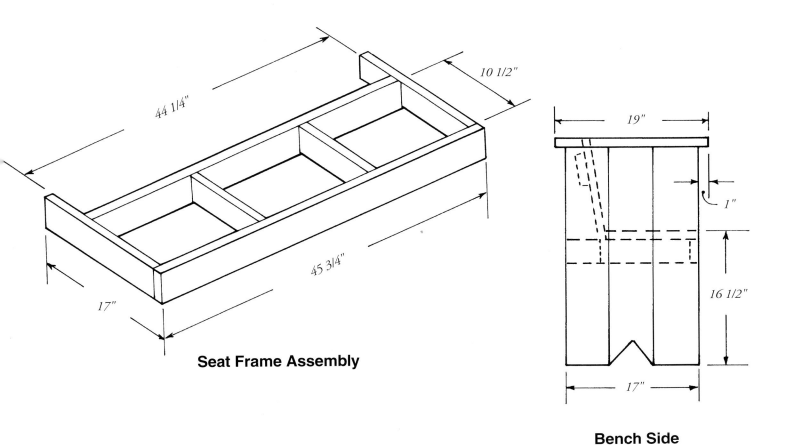

44 1/4"

10 1/2"

45 3/4"

17"

Seat Frame Assembly

19"

1"

16 1/2"

17"

Bench Side

KOI GARDEN CHAIR

Created By Kathi Malarchuk

This wooden garden chair is "stamped," a very quick and easy way to add decoration to your garden. Use this design to spice up an old faded chair or add a touch of color and creativity to your new garden furniture. This design could be adapted to decorate several pieces of furniture or almost any surface you dream up.

SUPPLIES NEEDED

Project surface:
Unfinished wooden chair

Paint:
Exterior latex paint, lime, satin or eggshell finish
Colored glaze, 2 oz.: new leaf green and plate blue

Brushes:
Large paint brush
Sponge brush

Primers & sealers:
Wood primer
Outdoor sealer

Foam stamp:
Koi fish design

Tools:
Sandpaper
Small paint roller
Sea sponge
Palette or disposable plates
Paper towels

HERE'S HOW

Prepare wood:
1. Sand wood, wipe away dust, apply primer, and sand again following general instructions for painting on wood.
2. Use large paint brush to basecoat chair with two coats of lime exterior latex paint, allowing to dry and sanding between coats. Allow paint to dry before continuing.
3. Wet sea sponge and wring out excess water until damp.
4. Pour new leaf green colored glaze onto palette and dip damp sponge into glaze. Blot sponge onto paper towels to remove excess glaze.

5. Lightly dab sponge over entire surface of chair. Pounce until you need to reload sponge. In order to achieve a definite sponge texture, avoid rubbing sponge on surface. Refer to photo #1. Allow to dry thoroughly.

Stamp design onto chair:
6. Pour small amount of plate blue colored glaze onto palette.
7. Load small roller with colored glaze and roll onto koi stamp. Refer to photo #2.
8. Stamp koi design onto chair, referring to photo for placement ideas. First, position stamp onto surface and use your fingers to press stamp, walking fingers around stamp to make sure entire stamp is pressed against surface. Refer to photo #3.
9. Lift stamp to reveal koi design. Continue stamping design onto chair. Refer to photo #4.

Finish:
10. Allow chair to dry 48 hours.
11. Brush or spray on outdoor sealer according to general instructions for painting wood. 🐝

1

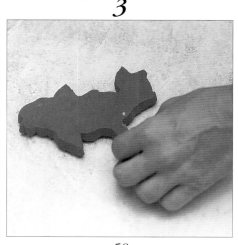

2

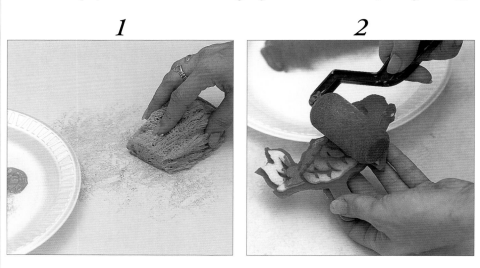

3

4

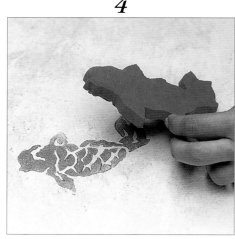

SOUTHERN DOGWOOD WATERING CAN

Created By Chris Stokes

Make sure that every garden accessory reflects the beauty of the garden with simple decorative painting designs such as this one. You can paint this design on an antique or new watering can or adapt it to other garden accessories.

SUPPLIES NEEDED

Project surface:
Watering can, 11" tall

Paint:
Acrylic craft paint: licorice, fresh foliage, wicker white, tapioca, harvest gold, raspberry wine, southern pine, milkshake, burnt umber, blue ribbon

Brushes:
1/4" stencil brush
#8 flat brush
#5 round brush
1/2" whisk brush
6/0 liner brush

Primers & sealers:
Rust inhibitive oil base primer
Outdoor sealer

Tools:
Cloth
Chalk, for sketching design
Graphite transfer paper, for transferring design
Tarnish remover, if necessary
0000 steel wool & denatured alcohol, for removing lacquer finish if necessary
Rubber gloves & safety glasses, for removing lacquer finish if necessary
Wire brush & sandpaper, for removing rust if necessary

Painting patterns on page 62

HERE'S HOW

Prepare metal:
1. Determine if the surface has a lacquered finish by running the edge of a razor blade over the surface. If small translucent flakes fall off, the surface has a lacquered finish that must be removed before painting.
2. If necessary, remove lacquer coating by using a piece of 0000 steel wool dipped in denatured alcohol. Clean the surface with cloth and denatured alcohol. Wear rubber gloves and protective glasses. Also be sure to work in a well-ventilated area.
3. Remove rust or flaking paint from watering can with a wire brush. Use metal sandpaper to further remove rust and smooth metal surface.
4. Use a tarnish remover to clean brass, copper, or silver before painting.
5. Apply two coats of rust inhibitive oil base primer to watering can. This is available in spray cans or paint containers. If painting on, use inexpensive sponge brushes to apply. Allow primer to dry according to manufacturer's directions.
6. To antique the surface, paint entire watering can with licorice paint. While paint is still wet, use a damp cloth to wipe off most of the paint, allowing paint to remain on edges.

Plan and transfer design:
7. Plan the placement of the design, referring to the photo.
8. Sketch the design free-hand with chalk or transfer the design using graphite transfer paper.

Paint design:
Refer to the painting worksheet on page 63.
9. Load #5 round brush with burnt umber and licorice to paint branches. Highlight with tapioca.
10. Using 1/2 inch whisk, paint nest using light pressure and mixes of harvest gold and burnt umber. Use licorice inside the nest and the darker side. Add details to nest with a liner brush.
11. Paint eggs using #8 flat brush, double-loaded with blue ribbon and tapioca.
12. Doubleload #8 flat brush with milkshake and tapioca to paint dogwood petals.
13. Float raspberry wine on tips of petals.
14. Float southern pine around centers of petals.
15. Doubleload a small stencil brush with southern pine and a touch of raspberry wine + fresh foliage to dab on centers.
16. Use handle end of brush to dot center with fresh foliage and a touch of tapioca.
17. Use handle end of brush to dot raspberry wine and touches of tapioca to create berries.

Finish:
18. Paint handle and spout with raspberry wine and touches of milkshake. Allow to dry.
19. After all paint has dried, you should seal your project for protection against the weather and use. Apply at least two coats of either a spray or brush-on sealer that is made for outdoor use. Follow manufacturer's instructions. 🐝

Painting Pattern — Southern Dogwood Watering Can

Actual Size

Pansies and Bird's Nest

Top Petals:
Double load #10 and #12 flat with Sunny Yellow and Touch of True Burgundy/Titanium White

Bottom Petals:
Periwinkle + Midnight Blue

Leaves:
Southern Pine + Sunny Yellow + Tapioca. Pickup touches of Burnt Umber and True Burgundy as you paint. Wiggle brush. Keep brush well-loaded with paint.

Dogwood:
Double load #8 flat with Milkshake + Tapioca. Float Raspberry Wine tips.

Nest:
Use 1/2" wisk - load with inky Burnt Umber + Harvest Gold.

Eggs:
Double load with Blue Ribbon + Tapioca.

Center is licorice - line brush detail

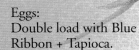

PRETTY PANSY GARDEN CHAIR

Created By Chris Stokes

Picture this small little chair out amidst the flowers, surrounded by beautiful colors, while contributing some beauty of its own!

SUPPLIES NEEDED

Project surface:
Wooden slat-bottom ladder-back chair
Wooden cardinal cut-out, life-size

Paint:
Exterior latex paint, beige, satin or eggshell finish
Acrylic craft paint: licorice, periwinkle, southern pine, burnt umber, dioxazine purple, cotton candy, apple spice, sunny yellow, tapioca, green forest, true burgundy, titanium white, midnight

Brushes:
1" sponge brushes
1" stencil brush
#10 flat brush
#12 flat brush
#5 round brush
#6 round brush

Primers & sealers:
Wood primer
Outdoor sealer

Tools:
Sandpaper
1" square cellulose sponge
Palette or disposable plates
Brush basin
Chalk or graphite transfer paper & pencil
Wood glue

Design Painting patterns on page 68.

HERE'S HOW

Prepare wood:
1. Sand wood, wipe away dust, apply primer, and sand again following general instructions for painting on wood.
2. Use large sponge brush to basecoat chair with two coats of beige exterior latex paint, allowing to dry and sanding between coats. Allow paint to dry before continuing.
3. Paint back of the chair and the front panels of the legs with sunny yellow acrylic paint.
4. Use a 1 inch square sponge to add checks of periwinkle acrylic paint to chair back.
5. Paint chair seat with stripes of periwinkle and yellow acrylic paint. Allow to dry.

Plan & transfer design:
6. Plan placement of design and sketch onto chair.
7. Load a 1 inch stencil brush with true burgundy, southern pine, and yellow. Dab onto surface on areas where you plan to paint design. Allow to dry.
8. Transfer design according to general instructions for painting on wood.

Paint stems & twigs:
9. Load #5 round brush with watered-down burnt umber and a touch of green to paint stems with a wiggling motion.
10. Load flat brushes with watered-down southern pine to paint leaves using a touch, press, pull, and lift method.

Paint pansies:
Refer to painting worksheet on page 63.
11. Doubleload #10 or #12 flat with dioxazine purple and cotton candy to paint some petals on purple pansies.
12. Doubleload #10 or #12 flat with dioxazine purple and licorice to paint center petals on purple pansies.
13. Load #10 or #12 flat with true burgundy, yellow, and a touch of tapioca to paint mauve pansies.
14. Load #10 or #12 flat with sunny yellow and a touch of true burgundy mixed with titanium white to paint top petals on blue & yellow pansies.
15. Load #10 or #12 flat with midnight and periwinkle to paint lower petals on blue & yellow pansies.
16. Load #5 round with licorice to paint throat on pansies.
17. Outline and add detail to pansies with tapioca.

Paint large leaves:
18. Doubleload #10 flat with sunny yellow + a touch of tapioca and southern pine + a touch of burnt umber to paint leaves. Add touches of burgundy on some leaves.

Paint cardinal:
19. Stain cardinal with watered-down apple spice. Float true burgundy and licorice on cardinal to shade.
20. Paint beak sunny yellow; shade with burnt umber.
21. Float licorice over face.
22. Highlight cardinal with apple spice and a touch of sunny yellow.

Finish:
23. Allow to dry 48 hours.
24. Brush or spray on outdoor sealer according to general instructions for painting wood.
25. Glue cardinal to top of chair with wood glue. Refer to photo for placement. ❧

See page 2 for overall view of chair.

FRUITS OF THE SUMMER STOOL

Created By Chris Stokes

This lovely stool will really come in handy around the garden! You can use it to display your other garden art,
as a plant stand, or as a stool to use while working in the garden.

SUPPLIES NEEDED

Project surface:
Wooden round stool, 12" high x 12" diameter

Paint:
Wood Stain, brown
Acrylic craft paints: fresh foliage, tapioca, green forest, burnt umber, raspberry wine, blue ribbon, taffy, school bus yellow, licorice, burnt sienna, apple spice

Brushes:
2" sponge brush
1/4" and 1" stencil brush
#10 flat brush
#5 round brush
Liner brush
Old scruffy brush
3/4" glaze brush

Primers & sealers:
Wood primer
Outdoor sealer

Tools:
Sandpaper
Palette or disposable plates
Brush basin
Old toothbrush or splatter tool
Graphite transfer paper & stylus or chalk

HERE'S HOW

Prepare wood:
1. Sand wood, wipe away dust, and sand again following general instructions for painting on wood.
2. Stain entire stool with a sponge brush and brown wood stain. Allow stain to dry before continuing.
3. Basecoat top of stool with tapioca acrylic paint using a sponge brush. Allow to dry.

Plan & transfer design:
4. Transfer design onto stool with graphite transfer paper or sketch free-hand with chalk. Refer to general instructions for painting on wood.

Paint outer vine:
5. Using a damp 1" stencil brush, pounce one corner of brush into a small amount of burnt umber. Pounce another corner into green forest, and another into raspberry wine.
6. Shade edge of stool using a circular motion with loaded stencil brush.
7. Load #5 round brush with watered-down burnt umber to paint vine along edge of stool.

Paint background leaves:
8. Load #10 flat brush with watered-down burnt umber, green forest, and raspberry wine.
9. Touch loaded brush to surface, press, and pull to a point to create leaves on vine.

Paint sunflowers:
10. Doubleload scruffy brush with burnt umber and burnt sienna to stipple on sunflower centers. Stipple on licorice to shade and school bus yellow to highlight sunflower centers.
11. Doubleload #5 round brush with burnt sienna and school bus yellow to paint bottom petals on sunflowers.
12. Load #5 round brush with burnt sienna, school bus yellow, and a touch of tapioca to paint top petals. Allow to dry.
13. Float burnt sienna on petals to shade.
14. Add details to sunflowers with taffy and school bus yellow.
15. Use handle end of brush to create burnt umber dots around sunflower centers.

Paint watermelon:
16. Load scruffy brush with apple spice and raspberry wine to stipple heart of watermelon.
17. Paint rind with green forest and a touch of burnt umber.
18. Highlight watermelon with fresh foliage; shade with raspberry wine.
19. Add seeds with licorice; highlight seeds with taffy.
20. Float taffy above watermelon rind.

Paint design- leaves:
21. Doubleload flat brush with green forest + a touch of burnt umber and taffy to paint some leaves.
22. Doubleload flat brush with green forest and fresh foliage to paint remaining leaves.
23. Add touches of raspberry wine to some leaves.

Paint grapes:
24. Doubleload 1/4" stencil brush with raspberry wine + a touch of blue ribbon and tapioca. Blend colors by pouncing brush.
25. *NOTE: You may wish to practice on your palette first.* Touch loaded brush to surface with light side up, twist to your left, and then lift.

Finish:
26. Load round or liner brush with watered-down burnt umber to add squiggles to design. Refer to photo.
27. Use old toothbrush or splatter tool to splatter surface with watered-down burnt umber.
28. Allow to dry 48 hours.
29. Brush or spray on outdoor sealer according to general instructions for painting wood. ❦

Design Painting patterns on page 69.

Design Pattern for Painting Pretty Pansy Garden Chair

Enlarge on copy machine @200% for size shown.

Chair Back

Chair Seat

Bird Cut-out

Design Pattern for Painting Fruits of Summer Stool

Enlarge on copy machine @143% for size shown.

CHAPTER 4

GARDEN SIGNS

Garden signs are a splendid way to greet visitors to your garden. Garden guests will realize immediately that your garden invites them to come enjoy. A sign that you have created and painted yourself will give you great satisfaction and be a marvelous reminder to you of your own hard work in the garden.

During the spring and summer, you can compliment the lovely colors of your garden with the delightful garden sign designs included in this chapter. In the winter months, bring a friendly reminder of brighter days with these instant garden enhancers. A wonderful aspect of these signs is that they can be personalized to express any message that you desire.

Cottage Garden Welcome
See page 72.

COTTAGE GARDEN WELCOME

Created By Linda Lover

Here is a wonderful example of how the designs in this book can be adapted to create a variety of projects. These instructions can be used to create the "Cottage Garden Welcome" sign or the "Sunnybrook Lane" sign on page 77.

SUPPLIES NEEDED

Project surface:
Weathered wood plaque, 15-1/2" x 18-1/2" x 1/2"
Weathered wood garden stake, 16" x 1-1/2" x 1/2" (used with the "Cottage Garden Welcome" sign)
2 weathered wood garden stakes, 12" x 1-1/2" x 1/2" (used with the "Sunnybrook Lane" sign instead of one stake)

Paint:
Acrylic craft paints or craft outdoor enamel: pine green, sprout green, fern green, sunshine yellow, foxglove pink, daisy cream, geranium red, summer sky blue, sunflower yellow, patio brick, pinecone brown, deep waterfall blue, lilac (can be mixed from geranium red and summer sky

Brushes:
10/0 liner brush
3/0 spotter brush
#4, #6, and #10 flat brushes
Old scruffy brushes (old, worn #6 and #10 shaders) for stippling
Sponge brush for applying primer

Primers & sealers:
Wood primer
Outdoor sealer

Tools:
Sandpaper & rag or tack cloth
Palette or disposable plates
Brush basin
Graphite and white transfer paper & stylus or chalk
Sponge
Saw, scroll, or jigsaw
Drill and drill bit to match size of screws
Screws
Masking tape

HERE'S HOW

Prepare wood:
1. Sand wood, sanding in the direction of the grain. You can leave the wood a bit rough and weathered.
2. Remove dust with a rag or tack cloth
3. Use a sponge brush to apply exterior primer to wood following manufacturer's instructions. Allow to dry.
4. Sand wood again to smooth the primer.
5. Remove dust.
6. Cut sign from wood plaque according to pattern.

Transfer design:
7. Use white transfer paper to transfer only the outline of the cottage and the lettering area onto the plaque. Reinforce design lines on plaque with chalk.
8. Place masking tape below the line marking the top of the lettering area.

Paint foliage & flowers:
NOTE: Foliage and flowers are pounced and stippled onto the surface. For this technique a paint-loaded old-worn out brush (scruffy brush) or sponge is used to simply "bounce" or "pounce" onto the surface. You do not need to transfer the design to paint these background features because they do not need to be exactly placed. Refer to the photo and pattern for general placement of background foliage and flowers.
9. Use sponge to pounce pine green on background area of design, avoiding cottage and lettering area on plaque.
10. Use large scruffy brush to stipple fern green around the edge of the pine green as a highlight.
11. Load the large scruffy brush with two colors, foxglove pink and daisy cream to stipple floral tree on the left side of the cottage, keeping the daisy cream to the outer side.
12. Load the large scruffy brush with lilac and daisy cream to stipple lilac bushes on both sides of cottage, keeping the daisy cream to the top.
13. Load small scruffy brush with sunshine yellow to stipple yellow flowers near lilac brushes.
14. Load small scruffy brush with geranium red and daisy cream to stipple in the floral clusters.
15. Load small scruffy brush with summer sky and daisy cream to stipple blue flowers.

Basecoat cottage:
16. Load #10 flat with daisy cream to basecoat cottage. Apply two coats, allowing to dry between coats.
17. Dip corner of flat brush in pinecone brown to shade under the roof area while blending into the daisy cream. Allow to dry.

Paint cottage design:
18. Use graphite transfer paper to transfer details of cottage design onto plaque.
19. **DOOR:** Doubleload #6 flat with pinecone brown and daisy cream to paint door, keeping pinecone brown to outer part of the door.
20. **WINDOWS:** Doubleload #4 flat with waterfall blue and daisy cream to paint windows, keeping the waterfall blue to the outside.

Continued on next page

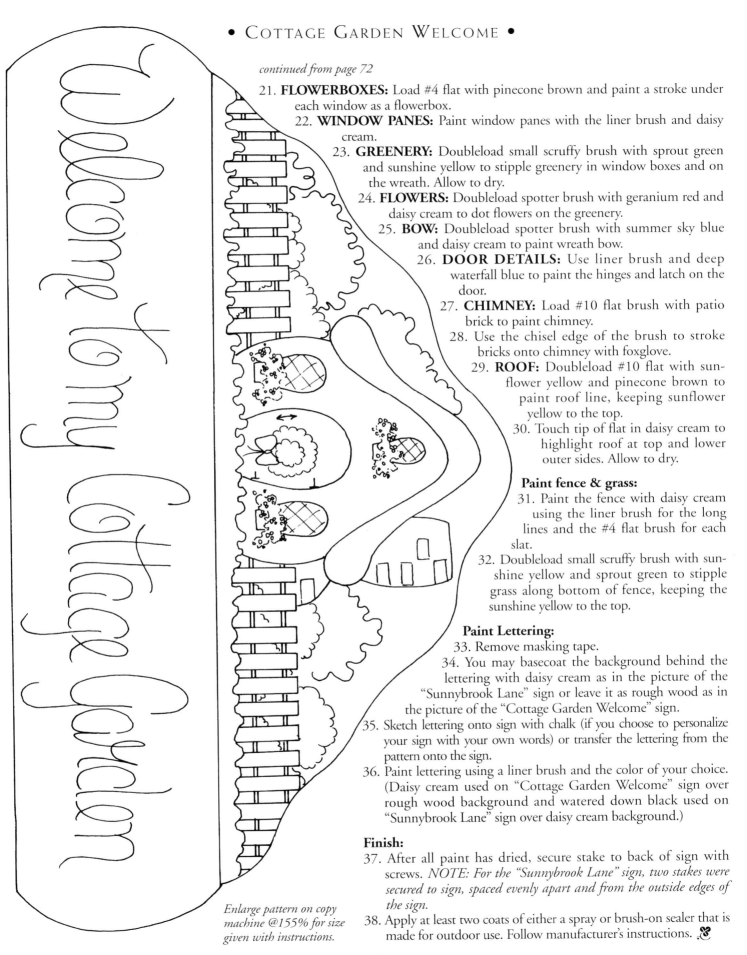

continued from page 72

21. **FLOWERBOXES:** Load #4 flat with pinecone brown and paint a stroke under each window as a flowerbox.

22. **WINDOW PANES:** Paint window panes with the liner brush and daisy cream.

23. **GREENERY:** Doubleload small scruffy brush with sprout green and sunshine yellow to stipple greenery in window boxes and on the wreath. Allow to dry.

24. **FLOWERS:** Doubleload spotter brush with geranium red and daisy cream to dot flowers on the greenery.

25. **BOW:** Doubleload spotter brush with summer sky blue and daisy cream to paint wreath bow.

26. **DOOR DETAILS:** Use liner brush and deep waterfall blue to paint the hinges and latch on the door.

27. **CHIMNEY:** Load #10 flat brush with patio brick to paint chimney.

28. Use the chisel edge of the brush to stroke bricks onto chimney with foxglove.

29. **ROOF:** Doubleload #10 flat with sunflower yellow and pinecone brown to paint roof line, keeping sunflower yellow to the top.

30. Touch tip of flat in daisy cream to highlight roof at top and lower outer sides. Allow to dry.

Paint fence & grass:

31. Paint the fence with daisy cream using the liner brush for the long lines and the #4 flat brush for each slat.

32. Doubleload small scruffy brush with sunshine yellow and sprout green to stipple grass along bottom of fence, keeping the sunshine yellow to the top.

Paint Lettering:

33. Remove masking tape.

34. You may basecoat the background behind the lettering with daisy cream as in the picture of the "Sunnybrook Lane" sign or leave it as rough wood as in the picture of the "Cottage Garden Welcome" sign.

35. Sketch lettering onto sign with chalk (if you choose to personalize your sign with your own words) or transfer the lettering from the pattern onto the sign.

36. Paint lettering using a liner brush and the color of your choice. (Daisy cream used on "Cottage Garden Welcome" sign over rough wood background and watered down black used on "Sunnybrook Lane" sign over daisy cream background.)

Finish:

37. After all paint has dried, secure stake to back of sign with screws. *NOTE: For the "Sunnybrook Lane" sign, two stakes were secured to sign, spaced evenly apart and from the outside edges of the sign.*

38. Apply at least two coats of either a spray or brush-on sealer that is made for outdoor use. Follow manufacturer's instructions.

Enlarge pattern on copy machine @155% for size given with instructions.

PAINTED SLATES

Created By Linda Lover

Garden signs can be painted on wood as in the "Cottage Garden Welcome" or on a variety of other surfaces. Painting on slates works well because very little preparation is needed, the slates provide a nice, smooth surface for painting, and the finished look is natural and earthy. Here are two delightful, different designs that you can use to enjoy painting on slates: "Flower Garden Slate" and "Garden Friends Slate."

GARDEN FRIENDS SLATE

SUPPLIES NEEDED

Project surface:
Slate with pre-drilled holes, 6" x 8"

Acrylic craft paints:
apple candy green, true green, cape cod blue, burnt sienna, maize, ultra black, ivory, adobe clay, harvest orange, light khaki

Brushes:
10/0 liner brush
#2 and #10 flat brushes

Cleaners & sealers:
Enamel surface cleaner & conditioner
Outdoor sealer

Tools:
Palette or disposable plates
Brush basin
White transfer paper & stylus or chalk
Textured sponge
Paper towels

Painting Pattern on page 78

HERE'S HOW

Prepare surface:
1. Wash slate with cleaner & conditioner, which works as a bonding agent. Allow to dry.
2. Load a dry sponge with apple candy green and dab onto slate surface, concentrating more color in the center of the slate. Blot sponge on a paper towel or palette, before sponging slate, if it contains too much paint. Allow to dry.

Transfer design:
3. Use white transfer paper to transfer design onto the slate.

Paint lettering:
4. Use liner brush and ivory to paint letters.

Paint greenery:
5. **STEMS:** Doubleload liner brush with maize and true green to paint stems.
6. **LEAVES:** Doubleload #10 flat brush with maize and true green to paint each leaf. Keep maize to the outer edges.
7. Tip the #10 flat brush in maize and pull the chisel edge up the center of each leaf to create veins.

Paint daisies:
8. **PETALS:** Load #10 flat brush with ivory and tip the corner of the brush in cape cod blue. Press the brush down at the edge of the petal, pull inward to the center, and lift. Keep the shading to the same sides of all the petals.
9. **CENTERS:** Tip the corner of the #10 flat in burnt sienna and paint the bottom of the flower centers.
10. Tip the corner of the #10 flat in maize and paint the top of the flower centers, blending the colors where they come together.

Paint bee:
11. Load round brush with maize to paint bee's body.
12. Load round brush with ivory to paint wings.
13. Use liner brush and ultra black to paint bee's face and body lines.
14. Highlight bee's face with ivory blended on the outer edge.

Paint butterfly:
15. **BODY:** Paint the body of the butterfly ultra black using the round brush.
16. Tip round brush in ivory to highlight outer part of body.
17. **WINGS:** Use #2 flat brush and adobe clay to paint the outer half of wings, pulling the brush from the outer edge inward.
18. Pulling paint from base of wings outward, paint inner half of wings burnt sienna. Blend the two wing colors where they come together.
19. Tip round brush in Ivory to paint design on wings.

Paint ladybug:
20. Use round brush to paint ladybug's body harvest orange.
21. Use liner brush to paint face and lines and dots on body with ultra black.

Paint leafhopper:
22. Load round brush with khaki to paint leafhopper's body.
23. Tip the round brush in ivory to highlight the back and wing.
24. Use liner brush loaded with ultra black to paint leafhopper's face; highlight face with ivory using liner brush.

Finish:
25. Apply at least two coats of either a spray or brush-on sealer that is made for outdoor use. Follow manufacturer's instructions. ✄

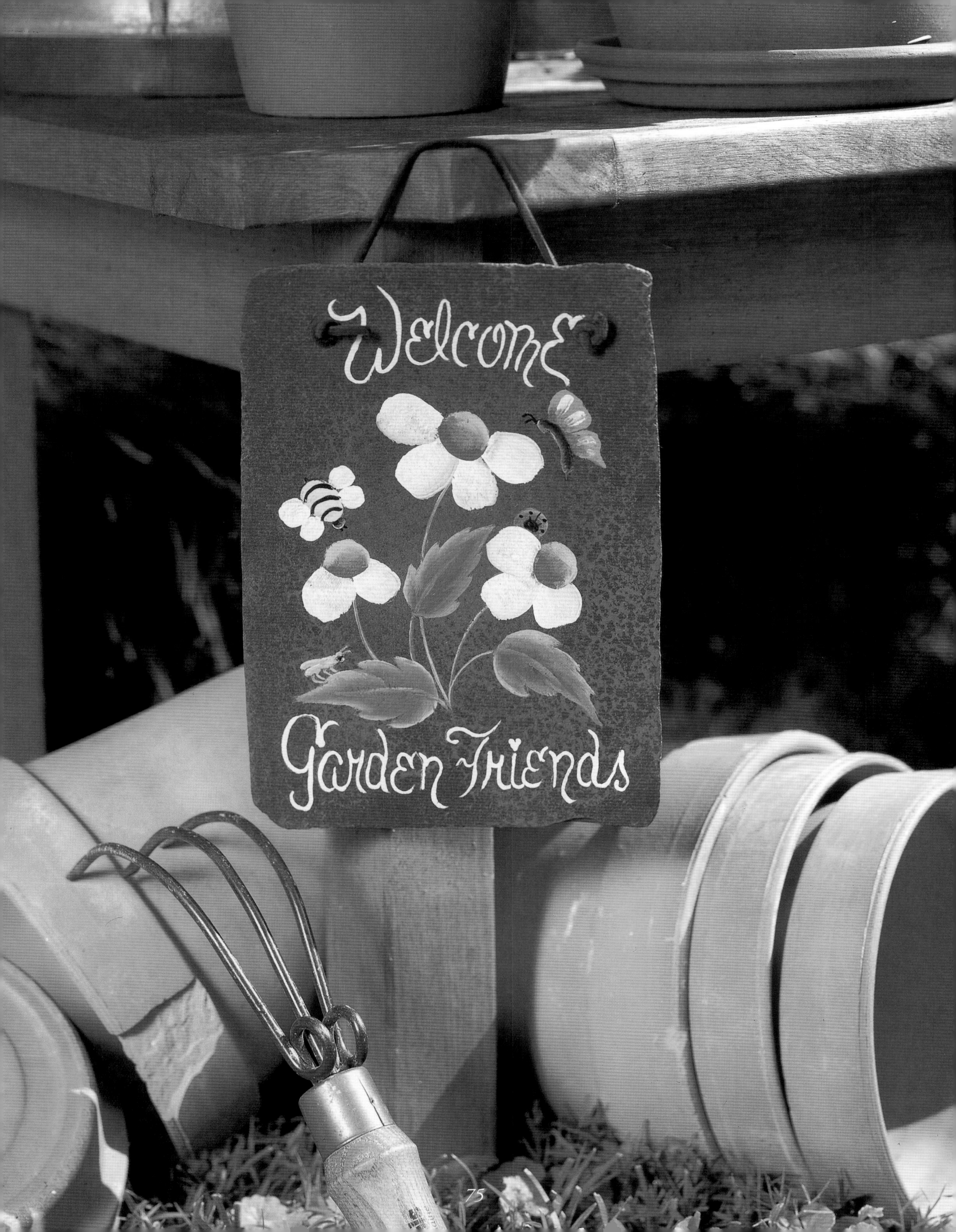
Welcome
Garden Friends

PAINTED SLATES
FLOWER GARDEN SLATE

SUPPLIES NEEDED

Project surface:
   Slate with pre-drilled holes, 12" x 6"

Acrylic craft paints:
   hunter green, true green, light blue, burnt sienna, maize, ultra white, cotton candy pink, light peach, tropical purple, eggplant, crocus yellow, dark goldenrod, fuchsia, mushroom, azure blue, red red

Brushes:
   10/0 liner brush
   #2 and #10 flat brushes
   Old scruffy brushes (old #4 and #10 shaders) for stippling

Cleaners & sealers:
   Enamel surface cleaner & conditioner
   Outdoor sealer

Tools:
   Palette or disposable plates
   Brush basin
   White transfer paper & stylus or chalk
   Textured sponge
   Paper towels

Painting pattern on page 79

HERE'S HOW

Prepare surface:

1. Wash slate with cleaner & conditioner, which works as a bonding agent. Allow to dry.
2. Load a dry sponge with light blue and dab onto slate surface, concentrating more color in the center of the slate. Blot sponge on a paper towel or palette, before sponging slate, if it contains too much paint. Allow to dry.

Transfer design:

3. Use white transfer paper to transfer only the background foliage design onto the slate.

Paint background foliage:

NOTE: Background foliage is pounced and stippled onto the surface. Stippling is a technique where an old scruffy brush is used to lightly pounce color onto a project. Keep the brush at an angle perpendicular to the surface. The amount of pressure you put on the surface with the brush will determine whether your painting will appear light and airy or solid and clustered.

4. **GREENERY:** Load sponge with hunter green and dab onto slate to sponge on the background greenery. Begin at the tree line and continue down halfway to the bottom of the slate.
5. Load large scruffy brush with true green and dab the corner of the brush into ultra white. Stipple along the top of the tree line. Also stipple randomly around the greenery. Keep the ultra white to the top.
6. **PINK FLOWERS:** Load large scruffy brush with cotton candy pink and ultra white to stipple on pink flowers. Dab a small amount of fuchsia on brush and lightly pounce over the pink.
7. **PURPLE FLOWERS:** Load large scruffy brush with eggplant and a small amount of tropical purple to stipple on purple flowers.
8. **YELLOW FLOWERS:** Load large scruffy brush with crocus yellow and a small amount of dark goldenrod to stipple on yellow flowers.
9. **MORE GREENERY:** Load large scruffy brush with true green and ultra white to randomly pounce greenery under the background foliage and on top of some of the flowers. Be sure to fill in the area inside the arbor. Allow to dry.

Transfer more of the design:

10. Use white transfer paper to transfer design of arbor, fence, and lettering onto slate.

Paint arbor & fence:

11. **ARBOR & FENCE:** Load round brush with ultra white to paint lines of arbor and fence.
12. **CLIMBING ROSE:** Load large scruffy brush with hunter green and crocus yellow to stipple on greenery of climbing rose. Allow to dry.

Continued on page 79

SUNNYBROOK LANE SIGN

This is a variation of the Cottage Garden Welcome sign. It shows how you can personalize the sign by painting your address in place of the welcome message. You can also paint on a slate instead of on wood. See instructions for the "Cottage Garden Welcome" sign for painting instructions.

GARDEN FRIENDS SLATE
Design Pattern for Painting

Actual size

FLOWER GARDEN SLATE

Continued from page 77

13. Doubleload small scruffy brush with red red and ultra white to stipple on roses.
14. **FLOWERS:** Doubleload small scruffy brush with fuchsia and cotton candy pink to stipple flowers inside the arbor.
15. Doubleload small scruffy brush with azure blue and blue light to stipple blue flowers beneath the pink flowers.

Paint lettering:
16. Load liner brush with light peach to paint lettering.
17. Line the right side of each letter with ultra white using the liner brush.
18. Paint the small heart at the end of the lettering with the round brush and light peach.

Paint pathway:
19. Doubleload #10 flat with mushroom and burnt sienna. Using the chisel edge, pull paint back and forth across the path.
20. Tip the corner of the brush into ultra white and highlight the path by painting thin lines and blending into the brown colors.
21. Tip brush into hunter green and using the chisel edge, pull paint along the sides of the path.

Paint foreground:
22. For painting the foreground, refer to photo and pattern for placement and coloring. Stipple foreground flowers onto the slate using either of the scruffy brushes and the following color combinations:
   red red & ultra white
   azure blue & light blue
   ultra white & light peach
   eggplant & tropical purple
   crocus yellow & goldenrod
23. Load small scruffy brush with fuchsia and cotton candy pink to stipple flowers along path.
24. Load large scruffy brush with true green and ultra white to stipple greenery below the flowers along the path and in the foreground. Stipple greenery wherever necessary to break up any paint that is too solid.

Finish:
25. Apply at least two coats of either a spray or brush-on sealer that is made for outdoor use. Follow manufacturer's instructions. 🐝

Design Painting Pattern

Enlarge pattern on copy machine at 145% for size given with instructions

CHAPTER 5

DOOR MATS

Doormats are a very quick and easy way to add decoration to your porch or pathway to the garden. You can purchase plain doormats in many different places including craft stores, garden stores, and home stores. The plain doormat is then very simple to decorate and paint. You can personalize it with your own special messages or favorite designs or follow the directions in this chapter to recreate one of the charming designs shown here.

The designs presented in this chapter are all very attractive, yet take only a few minutes to paint. Foam stamps, stencils, and acrylic craft paints are used to effortlessly and elegantly decorate these cheerful doormats. Seeing these splendid designs that you've created yourself to greet your feet will give you an extra spring in your step!

Field of Daisies:
See instructions on page 82

Trailing Ivy:
See instructions on page 82

Field of Daisies

Created by Kathi Malarchuk

For this design, you will use stencil brushes to easily pounce on the flowers. Only a few brush strokes are needed to create this delightful design. You do not need a pattern to paint this design. Simply plan the placement of your design and sketch a few oval and leaf shapes onto the mat, referring to the photo on page 80 for ideas.

SUPPLIES NEEDED

Project surface:
Woven exterior door mat, 23-1/2" x 35-1/2"

Paint:
Acrylic craft paints: dandelion yellow, canyon coral, forest green, black

Brushes:
Large & medium stencil brushes

Tools:
Palette or disposable plates
Brush basin
Charcoal pencil

HERE'S HOW

Plan and sketch design:
1. Use charcoal pencil to sketch large and medium-sized ovals onto mat, referring to photo for placement ideas. These ovals represent the placement of the daisies. Spread them out around the mat.

Paint design:
2. **DAISIES:** Load large stencil brush with dandelion yellow and pounce on the mat to fill in half of the ovals.
3. Load large stencil brush with canyon coral and pounce on mat to fill in the other half of the ovals. Allow to dry.
4. **LEAVES:** Load medium stencil brush with forest green to pounce tear-drop shaped leaves around daisies.
5. **STEMS:** Load medium stencil brush with forest green and pull across mat to paint stems and vines off leaves. Allow to dry.
6. **DAISY CENTERS:** Load clean medium stencil brush with black to pounce a dot in the center of each oval to create centers on daisies.

Finish:
7. Allow mat to dry for at least 48 hours before using. ✑

TRAILING IVY

Using foam stamps may be one of the fastest and easiest ways to add beautiful and colorful designs to your garden accessories. This handsome door mat is a marvelous example of how you can use stamping as a delightful way to add complimentary decoration to your outdoor areas.

SUPPLIES NEEDED

Project surface:
Woven exterior door mat, 18" x 29"

Paint:
Acrylic craft paints: forest green, real green

Foam stamps:
Ivy shaped foam stamps

Brushes:
#8 flat brush

Tools:
Palette or disposable plates
Brush basin
Charcoal pencil

HERE'S HOW

Prepare surface:
1. Use charcoal pencil to sketch diagonal lines on mat for the placement of the ivy, referring to photo for placement ideas. *NOTE: The mat shown was decorated on the reverse side.*

Stamp design:
2. Use flat brush to load stamps with forest green and real green.
3. Press stamps against the mat, stamping design along diagonal lines.

Finish:
4. Wash stamps immediately after use to prevent paint from drying onto them.
5. Allow mat to dry for at least 48 hours before using. ✑

Design Pattern for Painting

Repeat as needed to fill design area on mat.

TRIMMED TOPIARIES
Created by Kathi Malarchuk

Do you long for sculpted topiaries in your garden, but lack the time to trim them? Stencil them! Stenciling is a fantastic way to decorate your garden accessories with ease. You simple lay the stencil in place, tape it down, and then pounce paint onto the surface, filling in the cut out holes in the stencil. When you lift the stencil, you will be amazed by your own handiwork: neatly trimmed and attractive.

SUPPLIES NEEDED

Project surface:
  Woven exterior door mat, 13" x 23"
Paint:
  Acrylic craft paints: forest green, seafoam, black
Stencil:
  Topiary stencil
Brushes:
  Large & medium stencil brushes
Tools:
  Palette or disposable plates; Brush basin: Masking tape

HERE'S HOW

Plan placement of stencil:
1. Plan design to be stenciled onto mat and then decide where to begin stenciling.
2. Tape stencil into place at starting point.

Stencil design:
3. Load stencil brush with forest green and pounce over stencil to fill in the area for the topiaries.
4. Using same technique, stencil bases of topiaries with seafoam and trunks with black. Move stencil when necessary, taping in place each time. Allow to dry.

Stencil border:
5. Use masking tape to mark off a 1 inch border around the entire outside edge of mat.
6. Tear off small pieces of tape to mask off approximately 1 inch squares around border.
7. Stencil forest green in the areas between the tape.
8. Remove tape to reveal checks.

Finish:
9. Allow mat to dry for at least 48 hours before using. ❧

CHAPTER 6

BIRDIE BED & BREAKFAST

The flowers in your garden will surely attract the birds and the bees. However, your garden art can make your outdoor areas even more conducive to friendly flying visitors. Encouraging birds to make your garden their home will bring you a great deal of pleasure. You can sit outside and listen to their songs or watch their bright colors flutter across your yard.

The projects in this chapter use decorative painting to enhance the garden. The chapter includes beautiful garden accessories, such as a bird feeder, bird bath, and birdhouse. Each project will increase your enjoyment of the garden by attracting lovely birds and will also add its own characteristic charm to your garden.

A BIRDHOUSE TO BUILD

Welcome brightly colored birds to your garden with this cheerful birdhouse. For the most gratifying experience, build your own birdhouse, following the directions included here. If you prefer, however, you can buy an unfinished birdhouse and paint it using this clever design.

A BIRDHOUSE TO BUILD

Created by Jeff McWilliams

SUPPLIES NEEDED

Supplies needed for building your own birdhouse:

White pine boards, 1" x 12" and 1" x 6"
Cedar shingles, 1/4" thick, tapered
#4 finishing nails
Wood glue
Medium sandpaper
1-1/2" drill bit
1/4" drill bit
Drill
1/4" dowel rod

Paint:

Exterior latex paint, white, satin or eggshell finish for basecoating the house
Acrylic craft paints: sunny yellow, fresh foliage, tangerine, wicker white

Brushes:

1" stencil brush
1" paint brush

Primers & sealers:

Wood primer
Outdoor sealer

Tools:

Fine sandpaper
1/4" masking tape
1/2" masking tape
Measuring tape
Saw, scroll, or jigsaw

HERE'S HOW

Build birdhouse:

1. Cut out all pieces of the birdhouse body from 1 inch x 6 inch pine board, and the base from 1 inch x 12 inch board. Refer to diagram.
2. Sand wood pieces and wipe away the dust.
3. Assemble birdhouse body using #4 finishing nails and wood glue.
4. Use 1-1/2 inch drill bit to drill 4 holes in the front of the birdhouse for bird entrances. Refer to diagram for placement.
5. Use 1/4 inch drill bit to drill 4 holes under entrance holes. Refer to diagram for placement.
6. Cut 1/4 inch dowel into 4 pieces, approximately 2 inches long.
7. Insert dowel pieces into 1/4 inch pre-drilled holes to create perches. Glue into place.
8. Cut cedar shingles into varying sizes and assemble onto house using #4 finishing nails and wood glue.

Prepare wood:

9. Sand wood smooth and wipe away dust. Apply two coats of primer to birdhouse, allowing to dry and sanding between coats.
10. Basecoat birdhouse with two coats of white exterior latex paint, allowing to dry and sanding between coats. Allow paint to dry before continuing.

Paint design:

11. Place 1/2 inch masking tape on both roofs and the base of the birdhouse to keep paint from getting onto these areas.
12. Place 1/4 inch masking tape on the body of the birdhouse in a grid pattern. Use measuring tape to place the tape on the birdhouse in straight lines. Make sure that all vertical tape pieces are placed on the birdhouse with an equal distance from the sides of the house at both the top and the bottom. Make sure that all horizontal pieces are placed on the birdhouse with an equal distance from the top and bottom of the house at both sides.
13. Use 1 inch stencil brush to pounce sunny yellow acrylic paint onto the body of the birdhouse. Allow to dry.
14. Carefully remove all tape from the birdhouse.
15. Place tape on body of birdhouse along edges of center roof and base.
16. Load dry 1 inch paint brush with tangerine to paint the center roof of birdhouse, using vertical strokes.
17. Load dry 1 inch paint brush with fresh foliage to paint the base and perches of the birdhouse.
18. Use 1 inch paint brush to paint center of entrance holes with tangerine. Allow to dry.

Finish:

19. Remove all tape.
20. Apply brush or spray-on outdoor sealer to entire birdhouse. Use at least two coats.

Construction Diagrams

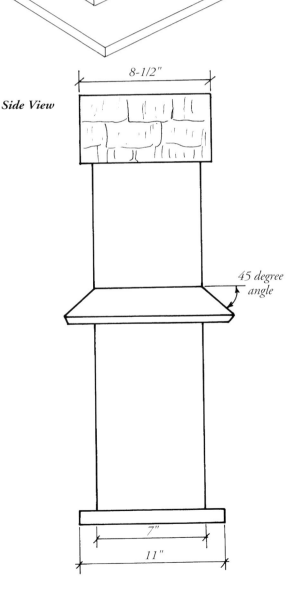

Cut from 1" (nominal) pine boards:
    2 pcs 26-1/2" x 5-1/2" (6" nominal) for sides
    2 pcs 29-1/4" x 5-1/2" w/ top edges angled 45 degrees for front and
    back
    1 pc 10" x 11-1/2" (12" nominal) for base
    2 pcs 9-1/4" x 2-3/4" w/ ends angled 55 degrees and 3 sides beveled
    45 degrees for porch roof
    2 pcs 11" x 2-3/4" w/ ends angled 55 degrees and 3 sides beveled
    45 degrees for porch roof

Cut from 1/4" diameter dowel rods:
    4 pcs, 2" long

Front View

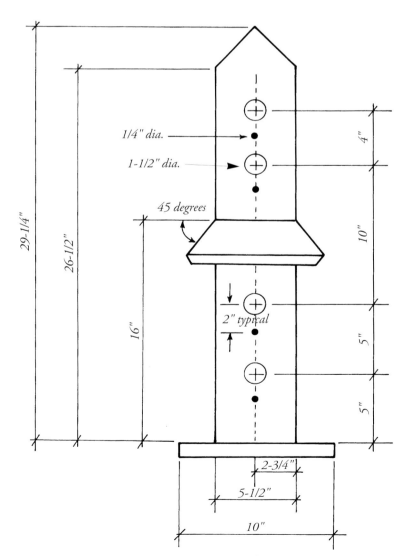

1/4" dia.

1-1/2" dia.

45 degrees

29-1/4"

26-1/2"

16"

4"

10"

5"

5"

2" typical

2-3/4"

5-1/2"

10"

Side View

8-1/2"

45 degree angle

7"

11"

HOLLYHOCK BIRD COTTAGE

Created by Chris Stokes

Chris Stokes painted this pre-made birdhouse with an adorable design to add color and detail to her garden. Then, she simply placed it in the ground. She says that bluebirds flock to it year after year.

SUPPLIES NEEDED

Project surface:
Wooden birdhouse (12" x 6-1/2" x 6") with stake (48" tall x 1-1/2" x 3/4")

Paint:
Acrylic craft paints: pink, violet pansy, true burgundy, burnt umber, licorice, moon yellow, mint green, winter green, tapioca, slate blue

Brushes:
Liner brush
#2 and #12 flat brushes
1/2" old scruffy brush or stenciling brush for stippling
1" sponge brush for applying primer

Primers & sealers:
Brown wood stain
Outdoor sealer

Tools:
Blending gel
Sandpaper & rag or tack cloth
Palette or disposable plates
Brush basin
Chalk

HERE'S HOW

Prepare wood:
1. Sand wood, sanding in the direction of the grain.
2. Remove dust with a rag or tack cloth
3. Use a sponge brush to apply brown wood stain following manufacturer's instructions. Allow to dry.
4. Sand wood again to smooth the stain.
5. Remove dust.

6. Basecoat birdhouse mint green.
7. Doubleload 1 inch sponge brush with true burgundy and pink to paint roof slats.

Plan design:
8. This design is very simple. You can sketch it freehand by looking at the pattern on page 92. Use chalk to sketch sign, lettering, door, steps, banister, and placement of swag onto front of birdhouse.

Paint design:
9. **DOOR & SIGN:** Basecoat door and sign moon yellow using #12 flat brush.
10. Float burnt umber over moon yellow areas to shade.
11. Outline door and sign with wintergreen.
12. **LETTERING:** Mix wintergreen with blending gel. Load #2 flat with wintergreen gel to paint letters.
13. **STEPS:** Paint steps with slate blue; shade with licorice and highlight with tapioca.
14. **GREENERY:** Load 1/2 inch stencil brush with watered down wintergreen and a touch of licorice to pounce background greenery along the base of the birdhouse. Allow to dry.
15. Load liner brush with watered down wintergreen and a touch of licorice to paint hollyhock stems.
16. Pounce greenery up the stems using the same green mixture as the stems and background. Allow to dry.
17. **HOLLYHOCKS:** Doubleload #12 flat brush with pink and moon yellow to wiggle petals onto some hollyhocks. Use same technique with violet pansy and moon yellow to paint remaining hollyhock petals.
18. Doubleload #12 flat brush with wintergreen and moon yellow to wiggle leaves on hollyhocks.
19. Stroke in front grass with watered down mint green.
20. Add dots to centers of hollyhocks with moon yellow.
21. **SWAG OVER DOOR:** Load liner brush with watered down burnt umber to paint twigs on swag.
22. Load liner brush with wintergreen. Touch brush to the surface and pull to create leaves on swag.
23. Load liner brush with mint green to add more leaves to swag.
24. Paint bow on swag with watered down true burgundy and a touch of moon yellow.
25. **BANISTER & RAILINGS:** Basecoat banister and railings with burnt umber; highlight with tapioca. Allow to dry. Shade with burnt umber.
26. **FLOWERS:** Basecoat pot on steps with moon yellow; shade with burnt umber.
27. Pounce greenery into pot with wintergreen.
28. Dot flowers on greenery with true burgundy and moon yellow.

Finish:
29. After all paint has dried, apply at least two coats of either a spray or brush-on sealer that is made for outdoor use. Follow manufacturer's instructions. ❧

Painting Pattern on page 92
See page 93 for closeup of Cottage

Design Pattern for painting Hollyhock Bird Cottage

Enlarge 140% for actual size

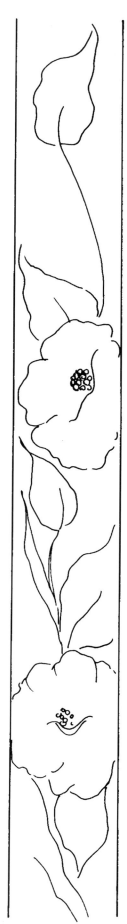

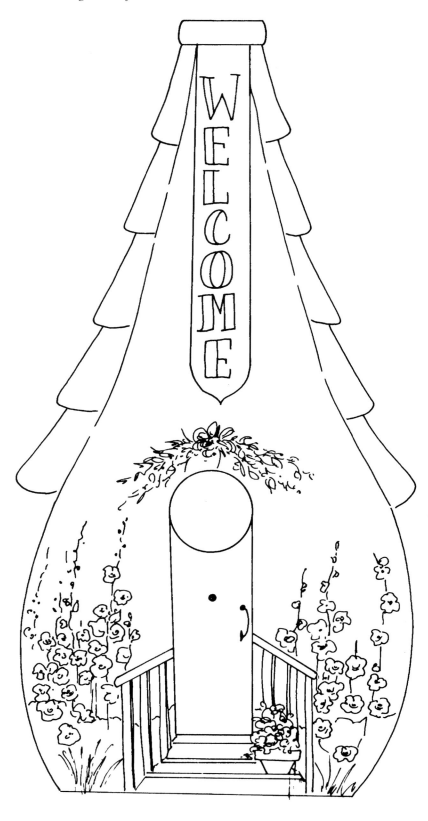

COUNTRY FEAST BIRD FEEDER

Created by Linda Lover

This is a fun and fast way to create a bird feeder that you can place on the ground, on your porch, or on a table. Its functionality combined with country charm will bring joy to both you and your bird friends.

SUPPLIES NEEDED

Project surface:
Terra cotta pot, 8"
Terra cotta dish, 10-1/2"

Paint:
Acrylic craft paints: mushroom, cape cod blue, country tomato, crocus yellow, ivory, ultra black, dark goldenrod, true green, chocolate, light khaki, hunter green, apple candy green

Brushes:
#3 round brush
#4, #8, #10 flat brush
#10/0 liner brush
1" wash brush

Primers & sealers:
Enamel surface cleaner & conditioner
Outdoor sealer

Tools:
White transfer paper & stylus
Tracing paper & pencil
Paper towels or rags
Egg carton, palette, or disposable plates

HERE'S HOW

Prepare surface:
1. Wash terra cotta pieces with enamel surface cleaner & conditioner, which will act as a bonding agent. Allow to dry.
2. Use wash brush to basecoat inside of dish and outside of pot with cape cod blue. Apply two coats, allowing to dry between coats. Allow to dry.
3. Basecoat the rim of the pot and the rim and outside of the dish with mushroom. Apply two coats, allowing to dry between coats. Allow to dry.

Transfer design:
4. Use transfer paper and stylus to transfer designs from the patterns given here onto terra cotta pieces. Refer to photo for placement.

Begin with the terra cotta pot; paint the background:
5. **HILLS:** Paint hills to left and right of mill light khaki using the #10 flat brush.
6. Paint hill on far right with Hunter Green.
7. Use liner brush to dot apple candy green dots on the khaki hills.
8. Paint "v" shapes on the hunter green hill with dark goldenrod.
9. **SUN:** Load #10 flat with crocus yellow to paint sun.
10. **CLOUD:** Load #10 flat with ivory to paint cloud.

Paint mill house:
11. **HOUSE:** Basecoat house country tomato. Allow to dry.
12. Coat house again with country tomato. While paint is wet, tip the corner of the flat brush in chocolate to shade under roof area and between the mill house and the waterwheel. Blend colors.
13. **FOUNDATION:** Paint foundation ultra black with the #8 flat. While the paint is wet, pick up mushroom onto the corner of the brush and paint the stones by flattening the tip of the brush on the surface and slightly blending the colors for each stone.
14. **ROOF:** Use #4 flat to paint the roof dark goldenrod. Allow to dry.
15. Doubleload flat with dark goldenrod and ivory to paint the roof again, keeping the ivory to the top.
16. **WATERWHEEL:** Use #4 flat to paint the waterwheel opening with ultra black.
17. Load #4 flat with chocolate and tip the corner into ivory to paint the waterwheel, keeping the ivory to the left.
18. Doubleload liner brush with ivory and chocolate to paint the paddles on the waterwheel.
19. **WINDOWS:** Use #8 flat to paint window openings ultra black. Allow to dry.
20. Use round brush to paint curtains cape cod blue.
21. Paint window panes with ivory using the liner brush.
22. Paint window box with ivory using the #8 flat brush.
23. Use #4 flat brush to paint shutters dark goldenrod. Allow to dry.
24. Use #4 flat brush to paint greenery in window boxes true green.
25. Add dots of crocus yellow for flowers in window boxes using the tip of the liner.
26. Paint tiny hearts on the tops of the shutters with country tomato.

Continued on page 96

COUNTRY FEAST BIRD FEEDER

Continued from page 94

27. Load liner brush with chocolate. Apply very little pressure as you pull the brush across the house to create board lines on the house. Use the same technique to paint board lines on shutters.
28. **CHIMNEY:** Use #8 flat to paint chimney chocolate. Tip the brush in ivory and line the bottom of the chimney rim. Blend the colors.
29. Tip the corner of the #8 flat in ivory and lightly press the corner of the brush on the chimney to create stones. Blend colors slightly.

Paint trees & bushes:
30. **PINE TREE:** Load #8 flat brush with hunter green to paint pine tree.
31. **BUSHES:** Use #10 flat brush to paint the bush next to the pine tree with a mixture of apple candy green and crocus yellow in a 1:1 ratio.
32. Paint the bush in front of the first bush with Hunter Green.
33. On the lighter bush, use the liner brush to dot the centers of the flowers with dark goldenrod and dot the petals with ivory.
34. On the darker bush, use the tip of the liner brush to add dots of dark goldenrod.
35. Paint the bushes on the other side of the house with the same colors and techniques as the first bushes. However, reverse the placement of the darker and lighter bushes.

Paint the foreground:
36. **GROUND:** Use the #10 flat brush to basecoat the ground apple candy green. Allow to dry.
37. **DUCKS:** Use the round brush to paint the large duck ivory.
38. Use the liner brush to paint the small ducks crocus yellow.
39. Paint all the beaks dark goldenrod, using the liner brush.
40. Dot eyes on the ducks with ultra black.
41. **WATER:** Basecoat the water with cape cod blue.
42. Doubleload the liner brush with ivory and cape cod blue to make a cluster of dots under the waterwheel.
43. Doubleload the liner brush with ivory and cape cod blue to paint water coming off of the wheel and to paint lines under each duck and in front of the cluster of dots.
44. **BIRDHOUSE:** Use liner brush to paint the post of the birdhouse ivory.
45. Paint the house dark goldenrod with the #4 flat. Allow to dry.
46. Add another coat of dark goldenrod to the house. While the paint is still wet, tip the corner of the flat brush in chocolate and shade under the roof. Blend the colors.
47. Use the round brush to paint the roof country tomato.
48. Use the round brush to paint the bluebird cape cod blue.
49. Paint the bluebird's beak chocolate using the liner brush.
50. Use the liner brush and very little pressure to add a dot of ultra black to the bluebird for an eye.

51. Use the #4 flat to paint the greenery at the base of the post with a mixture of apple candy green and crocus yellow in a 1:1 ratio.
52. Use the liner brush to dot the flowers on the greenery with crocus yellow petals and country tomato centers.
53. **BIRDBATH:** Use the round brush to paint the birdbath mushroom.
54. Use the liner to paint the goldfinches in the birdbath crocus yellow.
55. **LARGE APPLE TREE:** Load the #10 flat brush with apple candy green to basecoat the tree top on the large apple tree. Apply two coats, allowing to dry between coats. Allow to dry.
56. Use the #4 flat brush to paint the apples on the tree country tomato.
57. Load the round brush with hunter green to add leaves above each apple.
58. Load the #4 flat brush with ivory. Remove most of the paint by brushing onto a paper towel or rag. Use this dry brush to stroke in a reflection on each apple.
59. Paint the trunk of the apple tree chocolate using the #8 flat brush.
60. Use the liner brush to paint the rope hanging from the tree with dark goldenrod.
61. Doubleload the liner brush with ivory and ultra black to paint the tire hanging from the tree.

Paint remaining details:
62. **APPLE ORCHARD:** Use the liner brush to paint chocolate tree trunks on the apple trees in the background.
63. Use the #4 flat brush to paint each apple tree top apple candy green.
64. Add apples to apple trees with dots of country tomato using the tip of the liner brush.
65. **SHEEP:** Use the #4 flat brush to paint the sheep ivory.
66. Use the liner brush to paint the face, feet, and ears on each sheep with ultra black.
67. **FENCE:** Use the liner brush to paint the fence ivory.
68. **FOREGROUND FLOWERS:** Paint the leaves on the foreground flowers with a "v" shape using the liner brush and hunter green.
69. Paint the flowers with a "v" shape and an extra line using the liner brush and country tomato.
70. **RIM:** Use the handle end of the liner brush to add dots of country tomato around the rim of the pot. Allow to dry.

Paint the terra cotta dish:
71. Paint the ducks and flowers around the outside of the design as those on the terra cotta pot.
72. Paint the wavy line between the ducks with mushroom using the liner brush.
73. Use the tip of the round brush to dot flower petals in the

Design Pattern for Painting

Continued from page 96
center of the dish with ivory; dot the flower centers with country tomato.

74. Randomly dot dark goldenrod around the center of the dish.

75. Use the handle end of the liner brush to add dots of country tomato around the rim of the dish. Allow to dry.

Finish:

76. Apply at least two coats of brush or spray-on outdoor sealer, allowing to dry between coats. Follow manufacturer's instructions.

77. After all paint and sealer has dried, place the dish on top of the upside-down pot and fill the dish with bird seeds.

Enlarge pattern @155% on copy machine for size given with instructions.

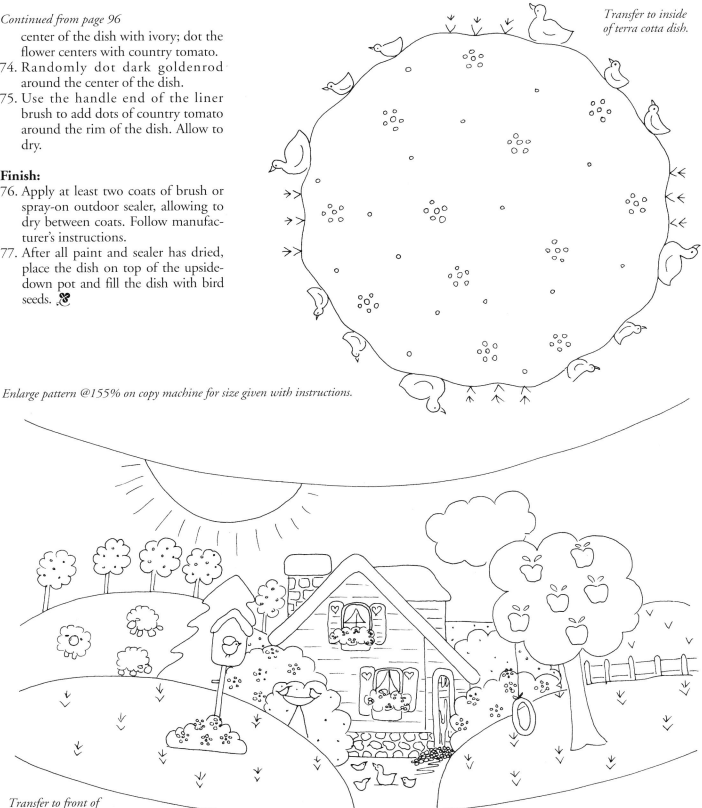

Transfer to inside of terra cotta dish.

Transfer to front of terra cotta pot, with pot upside-down.

MARBLE BATH

Created by Kathi Malarchuk

Bring the elegance of marble to your garden with this painted bird bath. The marbleized look is easily achieved by pouncing colors on the surface with a sponge. You could use this technique to enhance a multitude of outdoor decorations.

SUPPLIES NEEDED

Project surface:
Cement bird bath

Paint:
Exterior cement paint, white, 1 qt. for basecoating the bird bath
Colored glaze paint for creating marble look, 2 oz.: black, ivy green, roseberry, mushroom, russet brown, neutral
Neutral glazing medium, 8 oz.

Brushes:
Sponge brushes
Stencil brush

Primers & sealers:
Waterproof cement sealer to use as a primer
Outdoor sealer

Tools:
Sea sponge
Spattering tool or old toothbrush
Spray bottle & water
Feather
Palette or disposable plates
Scrub brush & muriatic acid for cleaning cement, if necessary
Safety glasses & rubber gloves, if using muriatic acid

HERE'S HOW

Prepare surface:
1. Clean dust, dirt, and grease off cement surface. Rinse off cleaners and allow cement to dry.
2. Use a sponge brush to apply waterproof cement sealer.
3. Apply two coats of white cement paint using a sponge brush. Allow to dry for 24 hours.

Create marble look:
4. Mix 1 part black colored glaze with 5 parts neutral glazing medium to make a gray color.
5. Use a sponge brush to wipe gray colored glaze mix over entire bird bath, allowing glaze to drip into crevices to create depth. Allow to dry.
6. Wet sea sponge and wring out excess water until damp. Dip damp sponge into ivy green glaze. Pounce sponge randomly over surface of bird bath.
7. Lightly mist bird bath with water using the spray bottle. Avoid misting too much so that water runs or drips. Use the stencil brush to lightly pounce over the misted areas. Allow to dry thoroughly.
8. Blend 1 part roseberry with 3 parts mushroom. Pounce mixed glaze onto bird bath with a damp sponge. Lightly mist with water and pounce with the stencil brush. Allow to dry.
9. Repeat sponging, misting, and stencil brush pouncing with russet brown colored glaze. Allow to dry.
10. Mix black colored glaze and neutral glazing medium to the consistency of ink. Use spattering tool or old toothbrush to splatter dots of inky black over entire surface of bird bath.
11. Dip feather into inky black mixture. Pull and push the edge of the loaded feather over the surface of the bird bath to create veins in the marble look. Work in small sections at a time.

Finish:
12. Allow to dry for at least 24 hours.
13. Apply at least two coats of a brush or spray-on sealer that is made for outdoor use. Follow manufacturer's instructions. ❧

MY BIRD HAVEN

Created by Chris Stokes

The beautiful flowers that make up this design will be a perfect compliment to the flowers of your garden. Show everyone how much both you and the birds love your garden!

SUPPLIES NEEDED

Project surface:
 Wood sign: 7-1/2" x 16" x 3/4"
 Wood bird cut-out: 1-1/2" x 4" x 1/4"
 Wood birdhouse: cut and assembled
  from piece 1-1/2" x 7" x 1/4"

Paint:
 Acrylic craft paints: cotton candy,
  periwinkle, harvest gold, moon yellow, pink, licorice, burnt umber,
  sunny yellow, tapioca, southern
  pine, blue ribbon
 Blending gel medium

Brushes:
 2" sponge brush
 Liner brush
 #2 and #10 flat brushes
 #5 extended round
 1/2" whisk brush

Primers & sealers:
 Brown wood stain to use as a primer
 Outdoor sealer

Tools:
 Graphite transfer paper & stylus
 Spattering tool or old toothbrush
 Palette or disposable plates
 Brush basin
 Sandpaper & tack cloth or rag
 Scroll saw
 Drill and bits

HERE'S HOW

Prepare surface:
1. Cut wood according to pattern. Sand wood smooth, sanding with the grain. Wipe away dust with a tack cloth or rag.
2. Use sponge brush to apply wood stain to all wood pieces. Allow to dry.
3. Use sponge brush to basecoat front of sign with moon yellow. Allow to dry.
4. Doubleload sponge brush with blue ribbon and moon yellow. Moving from the top down, brush across the top of the sign, blending the colors to shade the sky.
5. Doubleload sponge brush with southern pine and moon yellow, Moving from the bottom up, brush across the bottom of the sign, blending the colors to shade the ground. Leave the middle of the sign yellow.

Transfer design:
6. Use graphite transfer paper to transfer design from pattern given here onto front of sign.

Paint design:
7. **PATH:** Paint path with moon yellow and a touch of tapioca; float burnt umber on path to shade.
8. Load whisk brush with watered down southern pine and moon yellow to pull strokes up along the path to create grass.
9. Load liner brush with watered down southern pine and moon yellow and pull more grass strokes along the path.
10. Pounce pink and periwinkle flowers onto the path.
11. Use spattering tool or old toothbrush to splatter the path with watered down burnt umber.
12. **LETTERING:** Mix licorice with blending gel. Use #2 flat brush and gray mixture to paint lettering on the sign. Allow to dry.
13. **VINES:** Load #5 round brush with watered down burnt umber and southern pine to wiggle vines along the top of the sign.
14. **LEAVES:** Doubleload #10 flat brush with southern pine and moon yellow to paint leaves along vines; shade with burnt umber and highlight with tapioca.
15. **MORNING GLORIES:** Doubleload #10 flat brush with pink and cotton candy to paint pink morning glories. Use same brush doubleloaded with periwinkle and cotton candy to paint blue morning glories. Use same brush doubleloaded with sunny yellow + a touch of harvest gold and tapioca to paint yellow morning glories. Refer to photo for placement of colors.
16. Shade centers of morning glories with southern pine and a touch of burnt umber.
17. Add stamens to morning glories using the liner brush and tapioca with a touch of harvest gold.
18. Add detail lines to petals with watered down burnt umber.
19. Use a liner brush and watered down burnt umber to add distant birds to the sky.

Paint cut-outs:
20. **BIRD:** Paint yellow finch sunny yellow and harvest gold; shade with burnt umber and add details with licorice.
21. **BIRDHOUSE:** Leave birdhouse body stain color. Paint roof periwinkle.

Finish:
22. Allow to dry for at least 24 hours.
23. Apply at least two coats of a brush or spray-on sealer that is made for outdoor use. Follow manufacturer's instructions. 🐦

Design Pattern for Painting My Bird Haven

Enlarge 110% for size given with instructions.

Cut Wood Pieces:
    Cut sign from 3/4" wood using pattern
    Cut bird from 1/4" wood using pattern
Cut birdhouse front from 1/4" wood using pattern
Cut bird house room: 2 pcs 1-1/2" x 1-3/4" from 1/4" wood with one end of each beveled at 45 degrees
Cut perch 1" long from 1/8" wood dowel
Cut bird stand 2" long from 1/4" wood dowel
Cut birdhouse stand 3" long from 1/4" wood dowel

Drill wood pieces:
    Drill 1/4" diameter holes in sign to accept dowels for bird and birdhouse.
    Drill 1/4" diameter holes in bottom of bird and house.
    Drill 1/8" diameter hole, 1/8" deep in front of house to accept perch dowel.
    Drill 1/2" diameter hole, 1/8" deep in front of house to represent entrance hole.

Assemble sign:
  Glue roof pieces to top of birdhouse and glue perch dowel to front.
  Glue dowels to bird and house and then attach them to top of sign.

1-1/2" dia. x 1/8" deep hole

1/8" x 1/8" deep hole for perch dowel

HAVEN

CHAPTER 7

FLOWER POTS WITH FLOURISH

Most gardens are filled with flower pots. Show your creative genius and add interest to your garden by using hand-painted flower pots. Terra cotta is quick and easy to decorate. The designs in this chapter will give you some ideas to get started. Don't miss this perfect opportunity to combine functionality with decoration!

Pieces of Art Stucco Planter:
See instructions on page 106

PIECES OF ART STUCCO PLANTER

Created by Kathi Malarchuk

No one will be able to believe that you made it yourself! This artful planter (pictured on page 105) makes your flowers look even more beautiful. The design can be easily adapted so that you could make several pieces of garden art with this same technique.

SUPPLIES NEEDED

Project surface:
Cedar wood planter box, 30" x 6-1/2"
2 unfinished wood medallions, 1/4" x 4" diameter
1 unfinished wood medallion, 1/4" x 7" x 6"

Paint:
Colored gel glaze: moss green, new pine, russet brown

Sealer:
Outdoor sealer

Tools:
Sea sponge
Exterior stucco finishing mixture
Rag
Bucket
Paint stick
Paint trowel
Palette or disposable plates

HERE'S HOW

Create stucco surface:
1. Make stucco mixture following manufacturer's instructions. Prepare enough to be able to cover outside of planter.
2. Dampen exterior surface of planter with a sponge.
3. Apply 1/2 inch layer of stucco mixture to outside of planter using the trowel. Leave rough and keep damp.
4. Dampen back of wood medallions with a sponge.
5. Imbed wood medallions into stucco on front of planter so that stucco is flush up to sides of medallions. Refer to photo for placement ideas. Allow to dry for at least 24 hours.

Paint stucco surface:
6. Dampen sea sponge and dip into moss green colored glaze. Wipe over stucco.
7. Load sponge with new pine colored glaze and randomly pounce over moss green colored glaze. Also pounce on medallions.
8. Wipe medallions with a rag.
9. Load sponge with russet and pounce onto stucco, medallions, and remainder of wood planter.

Finish:
10. Allow to dry for at least 48 hours.
11. Apply at least two coats of either a brush or spray-on sealer that is made for outdoor use. Follow manufacturer's instructions. 🐝

FUN & FUNKY PLANTER

Created by Kathi Malarchuk

SUPPLIES NEEDED

Project surface:
Terra cotta planter with legs, 6" tall x 10" diameter

Paint:
Acrylic craft paints: white, lanier blue, real yellow, canyon coral, real green

Brushes:
#8 flat brush   Sponge brush

Sealer:
Outdoor sealer

Tools:
Pencil with new eraser
Palette or disposable plates
Brush basin

HERE'S HOW

Prepare surface:
1. If you plan to use your planter with flowers, you need to seal it before painting. Brush or spray on at least two coats of an outdoor sealer. Follow manufacturer's instructions. Be sure to coat both the inside and outside of the pot. Allow to dry.
2. Basecoat outside of planter white using the sponge brush. Apply two coats and allow to dry between coats. Allow to dry.
3. Basecoat the inside of the planter with lanier blue. Apply two coats and allow to dry between coats. Allow to dry.

Paint design:
4. Pour a small amount of lanier blue onto palette. Wet flat brush and load with lanier blue. Paint a wavy line near the top of the rim around entire planter. Add another wavy line near the bottom of the planter. Allow to dry and clean brush.
5. Pour a small amount of canyon coral onto palette. Load flat brush with canyon coral to paint spirals around middle of planter. Refer to photo for placement.

Continued on next page

Continued from page 96

Allow to dry and clean brush.

6. Load flat brush with real yellow to paint large dots between spirals.

7. Blend real yellow and real green in a 1:1 ratio. Dip pencil eraser into mixed color and dot around rim of planter and between spirals. Refer to photo.

8. Paint legs on planter with canyon coral.

Finish:

9. Allow pot to dry for at least 24 hours.

10. Apply at least two coats of a brush or spray-on sealer that is made for outdoor use. Follow manufacturer's instructions. 🐝

Tulips Terra Cotta

Created by Kathi Malarchuk

Supplies Needed

Project surface:
Terra cotta pot, 7" tall x 8-1/2" diameter

Paint:
Acrylic craft outdoor paints: real blue and white

Brushes:
Liner brush
Sponge brush

Foam stamp:
Tulip foam stamp

Sealer:
Outdoor sealer

Tools:
Small paint roller, 2" wide
Palette or disposable plates

Here's How

Prepare surface:

1. If you plan to use your pot with flowers, you need to seal it before painting. Brush or spray on at least two coats of an outdoor sealer. Follow manufacturer's instructions. Be sure to coat both the inside and outside of the pot. Allow to dry.
2. Basecoat entire pot real blue. Apply two coats, allowing to dry between coats. Allow to dry.

Stamp design:

3. Pour a small amount of white paint onto palette. Load paint roller with white paint and apply to foam stamp.
4. Press loaded stamp onto flower pot. Refer to photo for placement. Continue loading stamp with paint and pressing onto pot, placing tulips all around base of pot.
5. Wash stamp immediately after use.
6. Load liner brush with white to paint diagonal stripes around rim of pot. Refer to photo for placement. Paint diagonal stripes in two directions, forming diamonds on the rim.

Finish:

7. Allow pot to dry for at least 24 hours.
8. Apply at least two coats of a brush or spray-on sealer that is made for outdoor use. Follow manufacturer's instructions.

PERFECT POPPIES

Created by Kathi Malarchuk

SUPPLIES NEEDED

Project surface:
Terra cotta pot, 9-1/2" tall x 11" diameter
Paint:
Acrylic craft outdoor paints: dande-
lion yellow, raspberry, real red, white,
forest green
Brushes:
Stencil brushes
Stencil:
Poppy stencil
Sealer:
Outdoor sealer
Tools:
Stencil or masking tape
Palette or disposable plates

HERE'S HOW

Prepare surface:
1. If you plan to use your pot with flowers, you need to seal it before painting. Brush or spray on at least two coats of an outdoor sealer. Follow manufacturer's instructions. Be sure to coat both the inside and outside of the pot. Allow to dry.

Stencil design:
2. Plan the placement of the stenciled flowers. Refer to photo for ideas.
3. Tape stencil into place and begin stenciling the poppies with the following colors:
Flowers = 4 parts raspberry blended with 1 part white; shade with raspberry and real red.
Flower centers = dandelion yellow; highlight with white.
Leaves = forest green; highlight with white.

Finish:
4. Allow pot to dry for at least 24 hours.
5. Apply at least two coats of a brush or spray-on sealer that is made for outdoor use. Follow manufacturer's instructions. 🐝

POTTED IN MARBLE

SUPPLIES NEEDED

Project surface:
Terra cotta pot, 5" tall x 7" diameter
Paint:
Acrylic craft outdoor paints: seafoam, pacific blue, forest
green, eggshell
Sealer:
Outdoor sealer
Tools:
Sea sponge; Sponge brush; Palette or disposable plates

HERE'S HOW

Prepare surface:
1. If you plan to use your pot with flowers, you need to seal it before painting. Brush or spray on at least two coats of an outdoor sealer. Follow manufacturer's instructions. Be sure to coat both the inside and outside of the pot. Allow to dry.

Paint design:
2. Use sponge brush to basecoat entire pot with seafoam. Allow to dry.
3. Pour a small amount of pacific blue onto palette. Wet sea sponge and wring out excess water until damp. Dip damp sponge into pacific blue and pounce onto surface of pot. Allow background color to show through sponged color. Allow to dry.
4. Continue pouncing remaining palette colors onto the pot using the same technique. Allow to dry between colors.

Finish:
5. Allow pot to dry for at least 24 hours.
6. Apply at least two coats of a brush or spray-on sealer that is made for outdoor use. Follow manufacturer's instructions. 🐝

CHAPTER 8

WHIRLIGIGS
& WHIMSY

Creating and decorating garden art does not have to be a serious matter. A few cheerful, colorful, or playful pieces scattered throughout your garden can add a touch of frivolity or humor to your garden. This chapter highlights a few designs which allow you to break away from the seriousness of garden decoration and have a bit of fun.

UNCLE SAMMY

Created by Kay Riley

Bring a touch of folk art to your garden with this painted fence post. Uncle Sammy is the perfect piece of garden art to place in any empty corners of your garden that you haven't known how to fill. Make him the centerpiece on holidays and special occasions (don't forget Flag Day in June!)

SUPPLIES NEEDED

Project surface:
Cedar post rail, 68" tall
1/2" plywood for hat brim
1/4" dowel to secure hat and arms
2 dowels for arms, 1-1/4" x 18"
Pine wood cut in a circle for base, 1"
  x 12" diameter
Decorative flag

Paint:
Acrylic craft paints: skintone, nutmeg, tapioca, amish blue, barnyard red, indigo blue, wicker white, licorice, metallic gold, charcoal grey, acorn brown, salmon

Brushes:
Sponge brush
3/4" flat brush
#12 flat brush
10/0 liner brush
#3 round brush
1/2" angle brush
Stencil brush

Primers & sealers:
Wood primer
Outdoor sealer

Stencil:
Star stencil

Tools:
Sandpaper & tack cloth or rag
Transfer paper & stylus
Saw
Screws & screw driver
Drill and bits
Wood glue
Palette or disposable plates
Brush basin
Masking tape

HERE'S HOW

Construct Uncle Sammy:
1. Cut 12 inches off top of post for hat.
2. Cut plywood in a circle that is 3 inches wider than post diameter to make a hat brim.
3. Drill a 1/4 inch hole in the top of the post, through the plywood circle, and in the bottom of the hat.
4. Place a piece of the 1/4 inch dowel in the top of the post, through the plywood circle, and in the bottom of the hat to assemble the hat on top of the post. Secure with glue.
5. Cut a "v" shape at the bottoms of the 1-1/4 inch dowel arm pieces to create hands.
6. Drill 1/4 inch holes in the tops of the 1-1/4 inch dowel arm pieces (to connect the pieces to the shoulders) and a hole through the bottom of one piece (to hold the flag).
7. Cut one 1-1/4 inch dowel in half at a 22.5 degree angle. Glue dowel back together with the angle twisted to create an elbow.
8. Drill two 1/4 inch holes, one in each opposite side of the post, 10 inches below the hat brim to connect the arms.
9. Use 1/4 inch dowel pieces to connect the arms onto the shoulders, placing the dowels into holes on post and holes in tops of arms. Secure with glue.
10. Use screws to attach base to bottom of post.

Prepare surface:
11. Sand all wood surfaces smooth and wipe away dust with a rag or tack cloth.
12. Use sponge brush to apply two coats of primer to wood pieces. Allow to dry and sand between coats. Allow to dry.
13. Use transfer paper and stylus to transfer design outlines from pattern given here to post.

Basecoat the design:
14. **FACE & HANDS:** Use 3/4 inch flat brush to dry brush skintone onto face and hands.
15. **HAT & SHIRT:** Use 3/4 inch flat to dry brush tapioca onto hat above hat band and shirt. Lightly feather paint onto shirt collar.
16. Use #12 flat brush to basecoat cuff above hand with tapioca.
17. **PANTS:** Use 3/4 inch flat to dry brush tapioca onto pants. Do not fill in a small area under crotch and between legs. Refer to photo.
18. **VEST:** Use 3/4 inch flat to dry brush barnyard red onto vest.
19. **JACKET, SHOES, & HAT:** Use 3/4 inch flat to dry brush indigo on jacket, sleeves, shoes, hat band, and hat brim.
20. Paint buttons on jacket with metallic gold.
21. Allow all paint to dry.

Add details to design:
22. Use transfer paper and stylus to transfer design details from pattern given onto post.
23. **FACE:** Use #3 round brush to paint eyes tapioca in the corners.
24. Use #3 round brush to paint the bottom of each iris amish blue and the top of each iris indigo. Blend the colors.
25. Use #3 round brush to paint the pupils licorice.

Continued on page 114

UNCLE SAMMY

Continued from page 112

26. Use watered down licorice to paint detail lines on eyes with the liner brush.
27. Use the 1/2 inch angle brush to float licorice under each eyelid.
28. Highlight the eyes with wicker white using the liner brush.
29. Use liner brush to paint eyelashes licorice.
30. Float transparent acorn brown onto lips.
31. Float nutmeg onto facial shadows under eyebrows, above eyelids, around nose, under top and bottom lip, on laugh lines, above beard, over ears, in hollows of cheeks, and across forehead. Also float nutmeg on hands.
32. Float salmon on cheeks and lightly over lips.
33. **TIE:** Use #3 round brush to paint a bow around Sammy's neck with barn red.
34. **CUMMERBUND & LAPELS:** Load liner brush with watered down amish blue to paint cummerbund lines and to add piping to the lapels.
35. **STRIPES:** Use 3/4 inch flat brush to float barnyard red stripes on hat.
36. Use #12 flat brush to float barnyard red stripes on pants.
37. **EYEBROWS & BEARD:** Paint eyebrows and beard with strokes of charcoal grey and wicker white.
38. Use watered down wicker white to add a few lines to hair.
39. Use watered down nutmeg to add facial lines.

Stencil stars:
40. Place star stencil on hat band and tape into place. Refer to photo for placement.
41. Load stencil brush with tapioca and pounce over stencil to fill in star.
42. Lift stencil and move to next place along hat band. Continue stenciling stars all around hat band.

Finish:
43. Allow paint to dry for at least 24 hours.
44. Apply two coats of either a spray or brush-on sealer that is made for outdoor use. Follow manufacturer's instructions.
45. Place decorative flag in hole drilled into one hand. 🐝

Design Pattern for Painting Face

Enlarge pattern @155% for actual size

Design Pattern

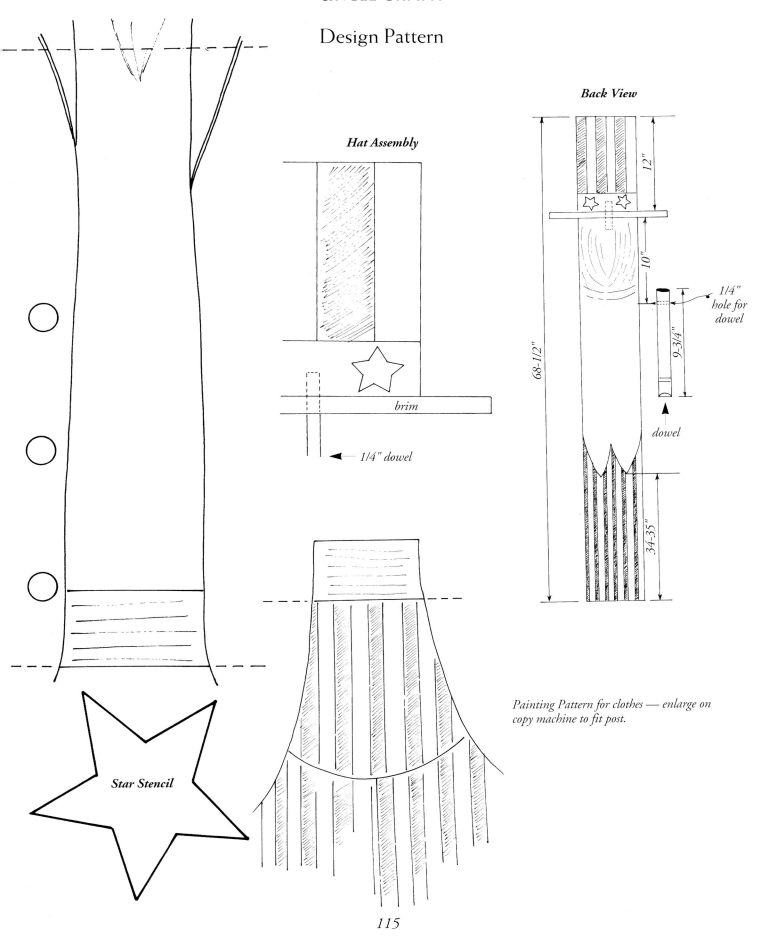

Hat Assembly

brim

← 1/4" dowel

Back View

12"

10"

1/4" hole for dowel

9-3/4"

68-1/2"

dowel

34-35"

Painting Pattern for clothes — enlarge on copy machine to fit post.

Star Stencil

A WHIRL IN THE GARDEN

Created by Lee Lindeman

This bright and playful sunflower whirls with the wind. It is almost as much fun to construct and paint as it is to watch and be mesmerized by its twirl.

SUPPLIES NEEDED

Project surface:
Pine wood, 1/4" thick, for cutting wood pieces
Wood slat, 1/4" x 1-1/8" x 21", to use for flower stem
15 wooden beads, 10 mm., split in half
2 wooden beads, 10 mm., whole

Paint:
Acrylic craft paints: yellow, brown, medium green, black, white

Brushes:
#2 filbert brush
#5 flat brush
#1 round brush
Sponge brush

Primers & sealers:
Wood primer
Outdoor sealer

Tools:
Sandpaper & tack cloth or rag
Palette or disposable plates
Brush basin
Tracing paper & pencil
Wood screw, 1-3/4"
2 washers to fit screw
Wood glue
Drill and drill bit
Scroll saw with tilting table
Screw driver

HERE'S HOW

Cut wood pieces:
1. Trace patterns given here onto tracing paper and cut out.
2. Lay traced pattern pieces onto pine wood and trace around the cut-outs with a pencil.
3. Use a scroll saw to cut out the wooden pieces. Cut the notch on the petals on an angle of 15 degrees.
4. Sand all cut edges with medium sandpaper and then with fine sandpaper. Wipe away the dust with a rag or tack cloth.
5. Drill a hole through the flower center, making the hole slightly larger than the wood screw.

Paint pieces:
6. Paint the petal pieces yellow, except the part inside the notch. Allow to dry.
7. Use round brush to add brown lines to petals. Refer to photo. Allow to dry.
8. Glue petal pieces around center piece.
9. Glue split beads on the center piece. Refer to photo for placement. Do not place any beads over the drilled hole.
10. Paint the center piece with beads, including sides and back, brown. Add a dot of black to each bead.
11. Paint the leaves medium green. Add black vein lines to leaves.
12. Paint the wooden slat medium green. This will be used as the stem.
13. Paint the bee's body yellow. Add black lines to his body and eyes to the face.
14. Paint the bee's wings white. Allow all paint to dry.

Construct:
15. Glue the leaves to the stem.
16. Place a washer on the screw. Put the screw through the hole in the flower center, working from the front to the back. Add a washer, a bead, and another bead to the screw on the back side of the flower center. Refer to diagram given with pattern.
17. Place the end of the screw into the flower stem and twist into position.
18. Glue the bee to the front of the stem.

Finish:
19. Paint the part of the screw that shows brown. Add a black dot to the center of the flower on the screw.
20. Allow all paint to dry at least 24 hours.
21. Apply two coats of a brush or spray-on sealer that is made for outdoor use. Follow manufacturer's instructions. ✺

Design pattern and diagrams on pages 118 & 119

Design Patterns for "A Whirl in the Garden"

Patterns to cut from wood

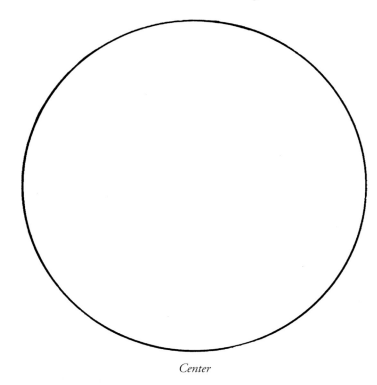

Center

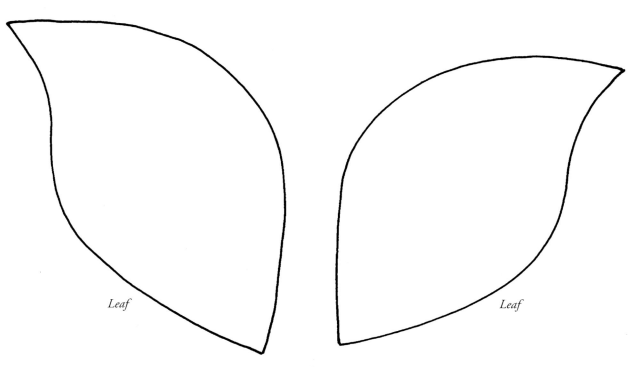

Leaf   *Leaf*

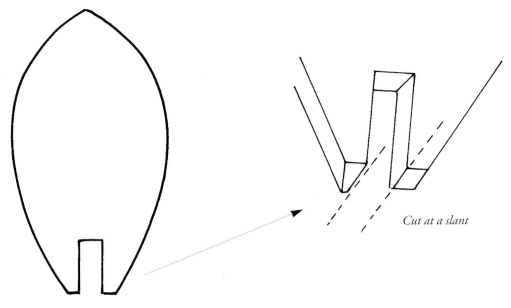

Cut at a slant

Petals, cut 12

Bee

Assembly Diagram

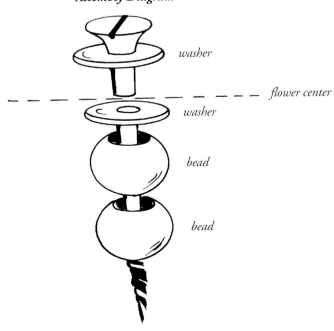

washer

flower center

washer

bead

bead

CHAPTER 9

ANTIQUES IN THE GARDEN

Creating your own garden art is not the only way to decorate your garden. A few well-placed antique pieces can remarkably increase your garden's beauty. An item that adds structure, form, or color to your outdoor area will create more interest and pleasure. Almost anything antique can be used: old pieces of fence, old furniture, rusted buckets or watering cans, or even old tin cups (consider painting them and using them as planters!). Collecting antiques for the home interior is very popular, but collecting them for the garden can be just as enjoyable. Worn, crackled, rusted, and patina pieces look radiant outside in the garden.

This chapter shows you a few ways to use antiques in your garden. You will find an array of exceptional ideas on how to present your antiques so that they are intriguing and attractive. You can use a wonderful rusted fountain as the centerpiece of your garden or use old pieces of furniture and fences to create decorative items in your garden to compliment and display your plants and flowers.

ENJOYING RUSTED IRON

When iron comes into contact with moist air, it reacts with oxygen and quickly begins to rust. The rust coating that forms on the iron is a pleasant color and looks very classic and natural in the garden. Sometimes iron pieces have been coated with a sealer or painted to protect them from rusting. For functional pieces, you may wish to keep them strong and stable and therefore, free from rust. However, for decorative pieces, a rusted or patina finish is often most desirable.

To achieve the rusted look, you will need to remove any paint or sealer that has been added to the iron. You can have paint professionally sandblasted from the iron. Then, the "naked" iron will naturally rust when left outside. The amount of water and salt in the air affect the color of the rust and the speed at which the iron will form rust. Therefore, creating a decorative item with iron that is in the process of rusting will bring you a bit of suspense and mystery. You are also insured of a unique decorative piece. ❧

An intricately decorated piece of rusted wrought iron fence (right) makes the ideal backdrop for ivy plants. The plants and the sculpted iron share a similar form of curves and swirls. When you find a piece of lovely iron fence you would like to have made into pot holders, ask a local metal shop to cut the fence into desired sections. A metal 4" ring was welded onto the bottom of the fence section to hold a pot (the metal shop can do this also). This plant holder makes a wonderful display for a fence or attached to an exterior wall of your home.

The beautiful rusted iron fountain (page 121) is the centerpiece of this lush garden. It invites solitude and reflection with its perfect balance and symmetry. The rusted color blends with the earth tones of the garden so that the fountain takes the center of attention with subtlety. Through the years, the fountain had been painted so that the lovely natural iron was covered with layers of paint, the last layer being white. After having the fountain professionally sandblasted to remove the paint, the iron was left to age and rust. Now the fountain truly looks like the antique that it is.